Entering the Chinese
e-Merging Market

Entering the Chinese e-Merging Market

Danai Krokou

BEP BUSINESS EXPERT PRESS

Entering the Chinese e-Merging Market

First published in 2019 by
Business Expert Press, LLC
222 East 46th Street, New York, NY 10017
www.businessexpertpress.com

ISBN-13: 978-1-94897-649-7 (paperback)
ISBN-13: 978-1-94897-650-3 (e-book)

Business Expert Press International Business Collection

Collection ISSN: 1948-2752 (print)
Collection ISSN: 1948-2760 (electronic)

Cover and interior design by Exeter Premedia Services Private Ltd., Chennai, India

First edition: 2019

10 9 8 7 6 5 4 3 2 1

Printed in the United States of America.

To all of you who dare and risk

China is going to be the world's largest consumption market, and that engine is going to drive the world economy. If you miss China, you miss the future.

—Jack Ma, Founder of Alibaba Group

Abstract

Over the past decades China gained the reputation of being the world's factory, focusing solely on manufacturing exports. This is about to change. The role of e-commerce is tremendously important in the context of the Chinese government's stated goal of relying less on exports to the recession-stricken West and focusing more on domestic consumption as a driver for further economic growth. This growth is largely underpinned by China's online population, which is currently the largest online population worldwide. This book is aimed at assisting Western entrepreneurs, SMEs (small and medium-sized enterprises) and investors to understand and ideally enter the Chinese e-merging market.

It is designed to work as a step-by-step guide to the online marketplace environment in China. E-Commerce is an easy, fast, and cost-effective way of entering the Chinese market compared to more traditional ways of entry. Chinese e-commerce offers great opportunities for high profit gains to Western companies seeking to do business in China without the hurdle of heavy upfront investment.

Entering the Chinese e-Merging Market provides a detailed overview of the Chinese online market and proposes different strategies available to foreign companies seeking to enter and remain competitive in this tremendously challenging and profitable market that is 21st century China. It provides practical advice, updated data, and relevant links for further reference that Western SMEs, investors, entrepreneurs, and business owners can use to establish their online presence in China.

Keywords

Chinese e-commerce; Chinese online market; Chinese e-tail; China social media marketing; China investment; China marketing strategy; China marketing

Contents

Introduction

Over the past decades, China gained the reputation of being the world's factory, focusing solely on manufacturing exports. This is about to change. The role of e-commerce is tremendously important in the context of the Chinese government's stated goal of relying less on exports to the recession-stricken West and focusing more on domestic consumption as a driver of further economic growth. By 2020, the Chinese e-commerce market will match the combined size of today's American, British, Japanese, German, and French markets. Foreign entrepreneurs and SMEs seeking to seize this opportunity need to be fully prepared to catch up with the rapid rise of e-commerce in China. With the highest number of Internet users worldwide—which in 2018 reached 772 million—China has overtaken the United States as the largest online retail market. Apart from increasing the overall consumption and driving economic growth, e-commerce is about to shape the entire Chinese economy in radical ways. As China's e-commerce landscape is gaining in dynamics and complexity, foreign companies will need to create effective strategies in order to ensure a successful entry. This book discusses exactly that. It explains and details the tactics that foreign companies need to follow to adapt their existing marketing and sales practices to the Chinese market and devise new, effective strategies that deliver real results.

China is officially going global. Part of this move into globalization has been an increasing focus on the country's soft power. China is now projecting a new image to the world through narratives that are very different from the ones the country projected in the past. Part of this new strategy is having Chinese talent, expertise, brands, and technology expand outside the country. Some of this soft power is being achieved through business partnerships and acquisitions. There is increasing cooperation with Western companies that are not just seeking access to the Chinese market, like in the past, but also want to access and learn from Chinese expertise, technology, and business methods in various areas. While in the past, many Western companies engaged in secret lucrative partnerships and activities in Asia, big names are no longer shy about declaring their Chinese activities.

Most importantly, Chinese e-commerce offers great opportunities for high-profit gains to Western companies seeking to do business in China without the hurdle of heavy upfront investment. This book provides a detailed overview of the Chinese online market and proposes the strategies that are available to foreign companies seeking to enter and remain competitive in this tremendously challenging and profitable market, that is, 21st-century China. The book provides practical advice, updated data, and relevant links for further reference. It offers suggestions and key models that foreign entrepreneurs and SMEs can use to establish their online presence in China.

The e-tail market in China is about to evolve quickly and in its own special way. The coming five years will be a crucial period for the explosive growth of a still nascent and very promising industry. Companies that fail to develop an active and targeted online strategy will miss out on key opportunities for expansion and growth. The ever-changing dynamics of this booming industry has created the need for constant monitoring of the competitive environment and the emerging needs of Chinese consumers. Companies capable of moving proactively within that landscape will be the uncontested winners of the coming years. With the right mix of determination, strategy, creativity, and flexibility, there is no reason why your company would not succeed in China.

Whether you are an entrepreneur, a startup, or an established company in your home country, and you are looking to expand in new territories, or simply a business struggling for survival in your local market, I want to assure you that there is tremendous potential for your product or service in China. Being an entrepreneur myself, I know what an important role inspiration, enthusiasm, and passion play in the early stages of any new venture. My aim is to guide, inspire, and motivate you in this new start. At the early stages, and especially if you are unfamiliar with China and Asian culture, you will very likely feel confused and frustrated. At this critical stage, it is crucial not to lose perspective and keep focusing on your objectives.

Doing business in China will teach you new ways of thinking and doing. If you want to succeed in China, you must be willing to risk, adapt, and grab opportunities as soon as they arise. Do not waste your mental energy criticizing situations that seem unacceptable to you, and always try to keep an open mind when you are faced with local business practices that might appear shocking or upsetting. Assuming you are as passionate as I am about doing business in China, I invite you to start exploring the Chinese e-commerce landscape.

China's E-Tail Revolution: Why China and Why Sell Online

China's astonishing economic growth has coincided with the Internet revolution. The combination of these two major driving forces is about to transform the retail landscape, and as a result, it has opened the way to a surge of technological innovation and entrepreneurial activities. In a country that is currently experiencing unprecedented growth in various sectors, online retail stands out for its remarkable potential for further growth. With more than 1.3 billion people, China still tops the board with the world's largest population and is currently the world's largest e-commerce economy. By 2020, the Chinese e-commerce market will match the combined size of today's American, British, Japanese, German, and French markets. Foreign entrepreneurs and Small and Medium-sized Enterprises (SMEs) seeking to seize the opportunity need to be fully prepared to catch up with the rapid rise of e-commerce in China. Chinese and foreign entrepreneurs are now being given the possibility to venture into this market with minimal start-up expenses and by gaining easy and low-cost access to a growing pool of potential customers. The growth of Chinese e-tail is already generating huge amounts of consumer surplus and has given Chinese shoppers living in remote areas of the country the possibility to access a much larger range of products than they could have imagined a few years ago.

Over the past decades, China has gained the reputation of being the world's factory, focusing solely on manufacturing exports. This is about to change. The role of e-tail is tremendously important in the context of the Chinese government's stated goal of relying less on exports to the recession-stricken West and focusing more on domestic consumption as a driver of further economic growth. This growth is largely underpinned by China's huge cyberpopulation, which is the largest in the world. E-tail has offered multiple tangible market incentives to Asian and Western entrepreneurs and SMEs operating in China by giving them the possibility to sell directly in the online retail market where economies of scale are less important than in traditional retail. Chinese e-commerce is growing fast, and it is unleashing a remarkable transformation in consumption patterns, technological innovation, logistics infrastructure, and productivity. Since the economic reforms of the late 1970s, international brands have been trying to sell their products to Chinese consumers. Together with local brands, they offer a wide range of products for consumers to choose from. This wide selection of outstanding products has made Chinese consumers increasingly demanding. On top of this, the arrival of new brands has created a rather fragmented market, which, again has resulted in fierce competition between brands making it hard for newcomers. The good news is that shopping has become an essential part of the government's national strategy for economic growth in China. Private consumption has grown at a rapid pace, and retail sales have grown at double-digit rates for years. Consumption is now the primary driver of the country's economic growth. China used to rely heavily on exports and manufacturing, but with a growing internal economy, improved economic infrastructure, a slump in international market demand, appreciation of the Yuan, and increasing labor costs, the importance of exports has decreased in recent years. China's transition to a more sustainable model is assisted by domestic consumption, technological innovation, and the service industry.

The term *Chinese market* is very general. In this book, it is used as shorthand for the sake of clarity and simplicity. The truth is that China is far from being one market. It is actually a group of 34 distinct markets, each corresponding to China's administrative divisions. Think about it. You would never sell to a Swedish consumer the same way you would sell to a French consumer. You would never sell to someone in rural Texas the way you would sell to someone in New York. They are different. By the same token, you would not sell to someone in Beijing the same way you would sell to someone in a second- or third-tier city of China. In a few words, there is no one-size-fits-all solution when it comes to marketing and selling in China. As diverse China may seem, however, one must be aware of two major uniting forces, especially when it comes to e-commerce and marketing: Chinese Mandarin and the rise of social media. These two uniting forces make business in China much easier and are the basic tools all companies need to use if they want to do business, advertise, market, and sell their products in China.

Mandarin

Mandarin is the official language of China. It was adopted nationwide in 1932. Its pronunciation is based on the Beijing dialect and is written using simplified Chinese characters. Whether you are in Shanghai, Beijing, Qingdao, or Harbin, people speak Mandarin in addition to any local dialect. This makes things much easier when it comes to communication, marketing, advertising, and doing business.

Social Media

Nearly everyone in China is not just on social media, but active on it. In the early days of social media, this trend was very appealing to people because social media was the only place one could connect with people from other parts of China and the world. Over time, social media became part of daily life. While in the West, everything happened gradually—when social media began to take hold, users could connect with friends and family using Facebook, search for information and the latest news using Google, and then login to Amazon to buy things in an affordable and fast way. In China, things happened differently. Several steps were skipped or shortened. Everything happened within a very short time. Platforms like QQ, WeChat, and Weibo started mushrooming and attracted huge numbers of users by making their services more efficient and expansive. Sites and applications included as many functions as possible and offered increasingly personalized features to keep users within their platform. For mobile users, features were designed to keep their phone memory and data usage at the lowest possible level. These social media platforms catered specifically to Chinese local customs. Features like red envelopes for Chinese New Year and quick gifts or payments to friends took off. Platforms are constantly testing new features that can improve the experience of Chinese users and increase conversion rates. The voice message feature is also widely used, so people can avoid spending time to type complicated Chinese characters.

The growth rate of e-tail in China has doubled every year since 2003. The increasing spending power of China's growing consumer class is a major driving force. From 2015 to 2025, the lower middle class in China is expected to rise from 290 million to 525 million people. The country's lower middle class is currently represented by households with an annual income of RMB 33,000 to RMB 50,000 (5,500 to 8,100 U.S. dollars). An average upper middle class household has an annual income of RMB 41,200 to RMB 120,000 (6,800 to 19,000 U.S. dollars). Although these figures might appear low, local price levels along with strict exchange rates must be taken into account. Hundreds of millions of Chinese people will experience a considerable increase in their disposable income in the coming 10 years. What is considered China's *poor* urban population has decreased from 92 million in 2010 to 62 million people in 2018, while households classified as *rich* have increased from one to 13 million. Considering this, it is no surprise that a great number of international companies want to enter a market with such a massive potential.

Research in 266 Chinese cities revealed that the growth of online retail has resulted in an incremental increase in the country's total consumption. Cities with higher online consumption rates are usually the ones with higher overall consumption. Another interesting fact is that consumption levels used to exhibit important variations across cities, but e-commerce is about to equalize these differences. Another interesting fact is that there is an expanding enthusiasm for online shopping among consumers coming from less-developed Chinese cities. Although the average revenue per person is much lower in these underdeveloped areas, the amounts spent online will soon become similar to those spent by shoppers from larger and more prosperous cities. This translates into a bigger wallet share for online purchases in developing cities, and the major reason for this is growing access to a wider variety of goods that cannot be found offline in third- and fourth-tier cities.

Apart from increasing overall consumption and driving economic growth, e-tail is about to shape the entire landscape of the Chinese economy in radical ways. For instance, competition has resulted in lower general retail prices. An additional advantage is that, by driving growth to other sectors, e-commerce has spurred the development of an RMB 84 billion (14 billion U.S. dollars) service provider industry, which e-sellers use to support their online trading activities. These services include payment systems, online marketing, advertising, logistics, warehousing, and IT services. Another positive outcome is that the success of e-tail has had an impact on the physical retail world. By offering a more effective retail service, the e-commerce industry is affecting a number of other sectors by urging traditional retailers to achieve a better coordination between supply and demand, which, again, is going to improve efficiency for the whole economy in the long run.

The Chinese E-Tail Ecosystem

In most developed countries, the retail industry has generally gone through distinct stages of gradual growth. Due to the fact that, in China, the retail market's coming of age has coincided with the digital revolution, its development has followed different patterns compared to other countries. Generally, after starting with local or regional industry players, the field is eventually dominated by a few national leaders. In the case of China, clear national leaders are yet to emerge. The top five retailers have less than 20 percent market share. If the startling growth of Chinese e-tail continues, the country's retail industry could skip the national stage and move directly from the local to the multichannel stage. Major online players have already emerged in the Chinese e-tail market. Alibaba and JD (Jing Dong) are among the top 10 Chinese e-tailers.

A large selection of products is critical for companies to generate consumer pull. With the traditional offline retail industry still fragmented and rather underdeveloped, e-tail has become very profitable, especially because the small online merchants can take advantage of local gaps, inefficiencies, and niches of unmet consumer demands. The Chinese e-commerce market can be split into two main groups: marketplaces and independent sellers. Marketplaces are clearly dominant, and they account for about 90 percent of the e-tail market, according to the latest figures. Marketplaces are third-party platforms. They provide a website for a large number of merchants to list their products. These platforms offer existing traffic flows and the necessary tools for listing products and setting up individual online storefronts. They can also connect merchants with reliable service providers to assist them with all aspects of their e-commerce activities such as customer service, logistics, and warehousing solutions. Their main revenues come from charging transaction fees and from selling online marketing services to e-merchants. In China, the majority of e-sellers choose to work with third-party platforms as a way to avoid heavy up-front investment and to access effortlessly large numbers of interested customers.

The dominance of marketplaces can be striking to many of you, especially because, in most Western countries like the United States, marketplaces account for a small part of the market. Due to the ease of entry and the low start-up cost, however, Chinese third-party platforms are generally the fastest and most cost-effective way of entry. Marketplaces have provided a powerful launching basis for microbusinesses, entrepreneurs, and SMEs. Taobao and Tmall, the largest online marketplaces in China, have encouraged the creation and growth of many local e-tail brands, known as *Tao brands*. These brands have become incredibly popular, thanks to Taobao's highly targeted online marketing campaigns and to merchants' attractive offerings both in terms of quality and price.

On the other hand, independent merchants who choose to set up their own websites or independent e-shops might be free from having to pay transaction fees to a marketplace, but they still have to invest substantial amounts of money to set up their own platforms, customize them to meet local needs and tastes, and in addition to that, they will have to be in charge of all associated operations that are required to secure large traffic flows. Such expenditure can be very costly and incredibly time-consuming. It is justified only if merchants feel confident enough in their ability to drive consumer traffic to their sites. In later chapters, I discuss the pros and cons of a standalone website, especially for brand companies.

Although C2C (consumer-to-consumer) accounts for a very small share of global e-commerce in most Western countries, in China, the C2C market is as important as B2C (business-to-consumer), accounting for almost half of total e-commerce transactions. Microbusinesses and SMEs are the typical sellers in most C2C dealings in China. As a matter of fact, the Chinese e-commerce market is profitable, except for independent online merchants. China is the global leader by combined B2C and C2C e-commerce revenues, generating almost one-half of the global online sales of products and services in 2017. Due to ongoing strong growth, China is expected to add several more percentage points to its share by 2021.

A few key aspects and current facts of the Chinese online market include the following:

- About 90 percent of the e-commerce industry is marketplace-dominated. Large B2C websites are leaders in most Western countries, but this is far from being the case in China.
- About 50 percent of the online market is C2C. In other countries, C2C shares are in the single digits.
- Despite the fact that Chinese e-commerce is still in its early stages, high growth has been achieved with relatively low investment.
- Overall, the e-tail ecosystem is highly profitable and marketplace-based companies are by far the best-performing market segment.

Transaction value of B2C online retail market in China: 1st Quarter of 2015 to 1st Quarter of 2018.

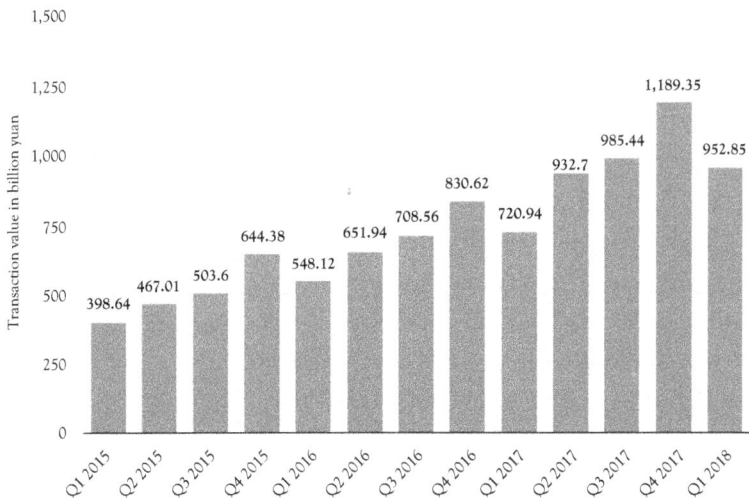

Structure of china's online shopping market by GMV
2012-2019

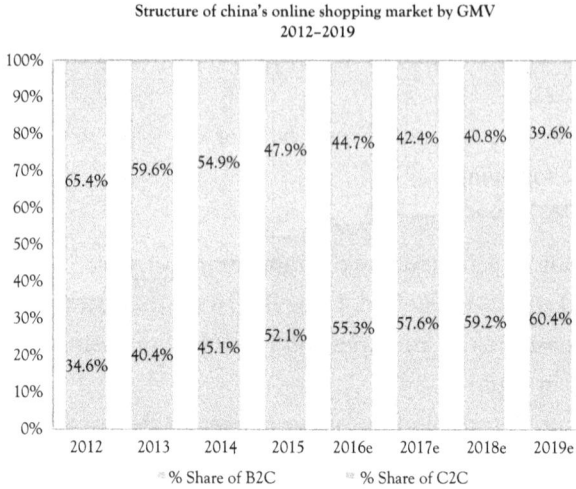

Source: The date were calculated based on the financial results published by enterprises and interviews with experts and iResearch statistical model.
*GMV: gross merchandise volume

China Online Shopping Market 2011-2018e

Source: iResearch Global Group, Fung Intelligence Center, company websites and interviews.

With the highest number of Internet users worldwide, which in 2018 reached 772 million, China has overtaken the United States as the largest online retail market. The Chinese e-commerce market has grown tremendously over the last 12 years, fuelled by the creation of third-party platforms like Taobao, Tmall.com, and Jing Dong (JD). On top of this, third-party payment systems, such as Alipay, have made Chinese consumers more confident with online shopping. A growing number of foreign SMEs who want to promote their products and services to a market with such a tremendous potential—while keeping their expenditure cost at the lowest possible level—regard the fast growth of e-commerce in China as an opportunity not to be missed. The most important factors influencing the growth of e-commerce across the country are broadband penetration, wide use of bank cards, and growing disposable per capita income. E-commerce, however, is far from being a mere substitute channel for purchases that would otherwise be made offline and should never be perceived as such. Its super-charged growth is the indicator of a radical transformation in consumer behavior; a transformation that is representative of the complex and dynamic economic landscape of the country in this beginning of the 21st century.

China's Leading E-commerce Platforms: Taobao and Tmall

To capture a share of this market's exponential growth, it is crucial to understand the factors that shape that growth. Alibaba's Taobao is the leading e-commerce platform in China. It was launched in 2003, and it now counts more than seven million active merchants. The great majority of Taobao merchants are small businesses and individuals. They can create storefronts and product listings on the platform. Payment services are provided free of charge. Merchants need to hold a Chinese bank account and an Alipay account to qualify for registration. Most Taobao sellers are intermediaries, often representing factories or selling goods from wholesalers. On Taobao, customers can find anything they can imagine. You will find both genuine and counterfeit products. So, the platform is best for goods that are not susceptible to counterfeiting. While Taobao does not have the same brand requirements as Tmall, their rating system and customer feedback ensure that bad sellers do not survive long. In terms of pricing, Taobao is as cheap as it gets. As it has more sellers than any other e-commerce platform and because these sellers often compete to sell the exact same goods, prices are very competitive. You are unlikely to find prices, anywhere and for any product, lower than what you will find on Taobao.

Taobao revenues come mainly from display marketing services, offered to merchants so that they can drive traffic to their virtual storefronts. Revenues come also from third-party marketing affiliate fees to acquire additional traffic, as well as from selling advanced software to merchants that helps them manage, upgrade, and decorate their online storefronts. Alibaba aims to increase consumption through e-commerce among the 600 million people that reside in rural China through the Rural Taobao Program. The company has established service centers in villages where rural residents can buy and sell products with the help of service center operators. The program not only helps village residents to sell their products directly to urban consumers, but also extends the reach of brands and manufacturers to those remote populations.

Tmall is a Taobao offshoot. The launch of Tmall by Alibaba in 2009 was part of the company's successful diversification efforts to expand from the Taobao fee-free, C2C model into the B2C market. Tmall is a platform where consumers can buy Chinese and international branded products. A large number of local and international brands and merchants operate their own stores on the Tmall platform. Alibaba revenues from Tmall come from annual upfront service fees, online marketing services sold to merchants, third-party marketing affiliates, storefront software, and commissions based on a pre-determined percentage of transaction value that varies by product category. Note that the right to sell on Tmall is reserved to companies that are legally registered in China and have a minimum of three-year market presence in Mainland China. Tmall currently dominates the Chinese B2C online market with a transaction value of more than 50 percent. The platform counts more than five million customers and over 70,000 brands. Tmall merchants are generally medium and large companies. The platform is used by more than 50 percent of online Chinese buyers. In terms of product quality and pricing, Tmall has much stricter requirements, and brands can only sell authentic and genuine branded products. All Tmall products are indicated with a Tmall seller badge that looks like this:

Following are the three main virtual store formats offered by Tmall:

- Flagship stores sell trademark products for which the merchant holds exclusive authorization.
- Specialty stores are used by merchants holding exclusive distribution rights to sell their products in China.
- Virtual stores offer merchants the possibility to reduce expenses and risk by testing the market before committing to a specialty or flagship store in China.

In spite of Alibaba's dominance of the B2C market, other important companies have emerged. Jingdong and QQ Buy are the second and third largest B2C online retail platforms in China, respectively. Competition has become fierce between these leading platforms and is expected to drive further improvement and innovation in delivery, after-sales service, and online payment methods. For instance, some emerging companies try to win customers away from Taobao by providing faster delivery and a more professional after-sales service. To compete with Taobao's customer service, many of these newly established companies have invested substantially in building their own logistics networks. For example, Jingdong has developed its own network of bike couriers and offer three-hour and same-day delivery in selected big cities in China.

Market share of B2C e-commerce platforms in China 2017

Alibaba Businesses

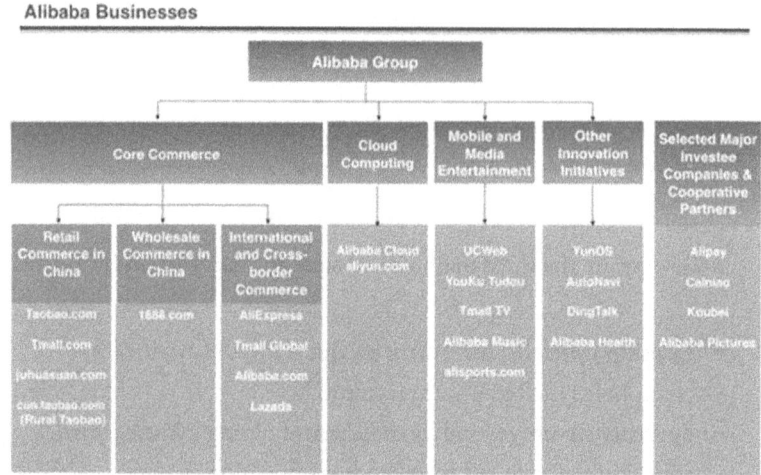

Source: Deloitte China Insights 2017, EUSME 2016–2017.

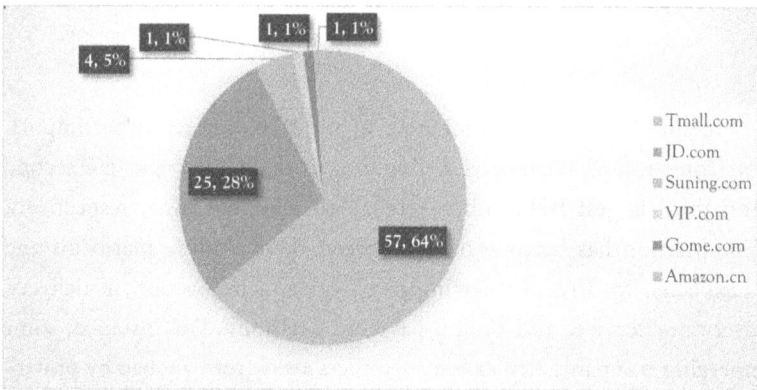

- Tmall.com
- JD.com
- Suning.com
- VIP.com
- Gome.com
- Amazon.cn

Source: Deloitte China Insights 2017, EUSME 2016–2017.

Online Consumer Behavior in China

Consumer behavior in China is complex and dynamic. China continues to urbanize very rapidly. It is estimated that 60 percent of the population will live in urban areas by 2020. This means that 100 million more people will become urban consumers. The per capita disposable income of these consumers has doubled since 2010 from about 4,000 U.S. dollars to 8,000 U.S. dollars in 2018. This reflects the extensive social, economic, and cultural transformations the country has been through over the last 30 years. With the coming of the Internet revolution, these changes have magnified and have shaped consumer needs and preferences in a way that would have been unthinkable a few decades ago. About 10 or 15 years ago, consumer behavior was much more contradictory and unpredictable. Launching a new product in the market used to be a much riskier undertaking. While the majority of Chinese consumers are not in the affluent or middle-income groups, there is a growing middle class that is fond of any sort of sophisticated imported goods. People in their late 20s and early 30s who live in urban areas are part of this growing middle class. They are better educated than their parents and tend to save less despite the fact that they earn sizable incomes. Although China's economic growth has been slowing down in the past few years, these consumers are optimistic that their earnings and living standard will improve and increase over time. Young consumers prioritize value and quality over low prices. In the past, price and practicality were the main criteria Chinese consumers considered the most when buying products. As they are now becoming more sophisticated and move from mass market to stylish, high-end products, Chinese consumers have higher expectations and have become very demanding shoppers.

China counts more than 700 million monthly active users on social media and 300 million online shoppers. While, for some, online shopping remains a trend and an occasional pastime, for many, it has become a lifestyle. Understanding this rapidly evolving audience is essential—on and off line. Keep in mind though that, while e-commerce is about to experience unprecedented growth, traditional shopping and marketing have not died yet. Shopping in malls and stores is still popular, and many Chinese people even travel abroad to buy luxury goods. Shopping tourism is, in fact, another major growing trend in China.

City Tiers

To facilitate a staged rollout of infrastructure and urban development, the Chinese government introduced a ranking system in the 1980s. Cities were ranked by tier according to the government's development priorities. Later, with a flourishing economy, this ranking started to take more criteria into consideration, including population, economy size, and political ranking. China's first-tier cities are among the largest and wealthiest. Beijing, Shanghai, Guangzhou, and Shenzhen are all key industrial, political, and commercial centers. Second-tier cities are mainly provincial capitals and coastal cities like Wuhan, Tianjin, Chengdu, Xiamen, and Chongqing. Third-tier cities are medium-sized cities in each province, while a number of smaller cities are grouped into fourth-tier cities.

Classification of cities in China by the development level*	
First tier	Beijing, Shanghai, Tianjin, Guangzhou, Shenzhen
Second tier	Nanjing, Hangzhou, Suzhou, Wuhan, Xi'an, Shenyang, Chengdu, Chongqing, Xiamen
Third tier	Jinan, Hefei, Dalian, Harbin, Changsha, Zhengzhou, Shijiazhuang, Fuzhou, Taiyuan, Urumqi, Qingdao
Fourth tier	Kunming, Nanchang, Ningbo, Guiyang, Lanzhou, Yinchuan, Nanning, Changchun, Baoding, Datong, Weihai, Shantou, Haikuo, Lhasa

* *These designations change from time to time based on rapid economic change and the weighting of different criteria.*

Present-day Chinese consumers regard shopping as a leisure activity. They do more online and offline research than their American counterparts before purchasing a product. They are demanding consumers looking for the highest-value product at the lowest possible price. Although Chinese consumers have a different purchasing behavior than their

Western counterparts, they are beginning to become more alike. There are, in fact, a few characteristics they generally value most: the quality and trendiness of a product, as well as the quality and rapidity of customer service and delivery.

Another growing trend that has been ingrained into the younger generation of Chinese consumers is the status-building value of a product. *Mianzi* is a very important cultural factor in China and plays a major role in both social and business dealings. The term literally means *face*, but the most accurate translation would be *personal honor*. This concept commonly refers to the good reputation a person gets when they make wise decisions by avoiding mistakes or embarrassing situations. People *give* face to others, who *receive* it, by showing respect or by giving compliments. Given the extraordinary importance Chinese people attribute to reputation, it is imperative that this cultural factor is taken into account in any company's marketing and sales strategy. Chinese consumers care a lot about the image they project to the outside world. Face—the primary currency of upward mobility—is rooted in status projection and generates societal acknowledgment for one's ability to scale the socioeconomic hierarchy. Younger consumers are particularly brand-conscious and have a special preference for luxury products that allow them to *build face* or *show off* to their peers. Luxury products are often considered an investment because they are likely to be made of higher-quality materials.

Who Is Buying?

As it has been already discussed, it is easy to see China as a single market, but a simple look at the population size and the country's geography is enough to notice that it is a lot more diverse. China counts 56 ethnic groups. Therefore, levels of wealth and consumer preferences vary widely. One major factor in consumer diversity is the huge gap in income levels among and within different areas. First-tier cities, the ones with the highest income levels, are situated along the coast of China, going up the coast past Macau and Hong Kong. Considering all these population variations, consumer behavior in China follows rather uncommon and unpredictable patterns. About 65 percent of the international businesses operating in China have admitted that they had to adjust their product specifically to the Chinese market to suit local tastes and needs. Therefore, to maximize relevance and trigger loyalty, global brands must embrace Chinese cultural and operational realities.

Chinese culture is traditionally collectivistic as opposed to Western cultures, which have developed more individualistic characteristics. Whereas Western consumers' sense of identity and self-worth is based on such characteristics as difference, uniqueness, and *standing out from the crowd*, Chinese consumers are community-oriented. *Crowd* is a word carrying positive connotations for them. The country has been categorized in the minds of many Western people as a *copy nation*. Chinese people like to copy, and they have proved to be very good at doing that. Their copying tendency is not merely limited to brands and products though. They copy trends and social behaviors. They like to copy each other. For Chinese people, being different and standing out means being excluded. Their identity and sense of self depend on how they are perceived by the group. If you want to be a member of the community, you have to follow certain practices and rules, and one of the major rules is harmonizing individual behavior with collective behavior. As a result, they tend to mimic peer behavior and usually follow what other people do, be it friends, family, or colleagues. The same applies to consumer behavior. In the later chapters, I explain the importance and ways of using local social media as a key online marketing strategy for creating virtual communities of e-shoppers.

Fashion-conscious young men and women belonging to the middle and upper-middle classes are usually the target market segment for most Western companies selling their products in China. If we try to define the average Chinese consumer in just a few words, we would describe a group of people belonging to the one-child generation, born between 1978 and 1990. This group represents approximately 300 million people. The e-generation is represented by younger consumers born in the 1990s. Those born after 1998 currently represent 260 million individuals. The one-child generation tends to be rather materialistic and shares a number of characteristics with Western consumers. Other behavioral aspects include the tendency to spend rather than save like previous generations used to do. Groups of young consumers follow current trends through the Internet and are more likely to spend large amounts on fashion, clothing, entertainment, and personal care items. Most Internet users—even those living in remote regions of the country—have broadband access, and mobile shopping is becoming an increasingly growing trend among them as well.

Young people are more likely to spend time and money online than older consumers. More than 90 percent of online shoppers are aged between 15 and 39 years. Most come from urban areas and have a monthly income of less than RMB 6,000 (989 U.S. dollars). About 29 percent are students, 18.3 percent are managerial and non-managerial white-collar employees, 17 percent are self-employed, and 11 percent are professional technicians. Female users account for almost 52 percent of all Internet users; they represented only 20 percent of the total Internet user population back in the early 2000s. While 3C (consumer, communications, and computers) products were aimed at male consumers a few years ago, the largest categories, mainly fashion and cosmetics, now target women. Chinese consumers generally opt for the lowest price and regularly compare prices between virtual and physical stores before purchasing. This is why, timely responsiveness to daily price changes is paramount for companies to keep competitive on and offline.

Emerging Consumer Groups

Chinese consumers are changing all the time. They are quite unpredictable. So are consumer groups. Emerging consumer groups introduce new consumption trends, and their growing influence must be constantly monitored.

Seniors

As an aging society, China enjoys a relatively high life expectancy and a low birth rate. Thanks to higher living standards and advanced medical solutions, the average life expectancy has reached 75.7 years. It is, in fact, these higher living standards that led to a reduction in birth rates with the implementation of the one-child policy in the late 1970s. The government has recently moved to a policy allowing two children in some circumstances. However, China is still facing the problem of an aging population. It is estimated that, by 2050, the number of Chinese citizens over the age of 65 years is expected to reach 329 million. The growing population of senior citizens makes them an emerging group in the foreseeable future. Modern seniors are more willing to pursue a lavish lifestyle than previous generations. They are cultivating their own interests and enjoy traveling. About 25 percent of the Chinese travelers in 2017 were 60 years or above. These numbers reflect the huge potential for special services, such as travel packages designed for senior travelers. Health products and medical services are also in high demand by this group of consumers.

Single Young People

The economic growth in China has fostered development in education. Children are told from a young age that they need to study hard to get a well-paying job and secure a good living. In fact, since the late 1970s, education levels have continued to improve. Defying tradition, young Chinese are increasingly postponing marriage and childbearing. A big number are aiming for higher education levels, career advancement, and higher social status, while others think it costs too much to get married. Young Chinese are, therefore, more willing to stay single and spend time and money on themselves than their parents and grandparents. According to the estimates, the number of single Chinese adults has already reached 200 million. A number that is equivalent to the combined populations of Russia and the United Kingdom. Because they do not need to take care of a family, they can spend more time and money on entertainment and recreation with friends and colleagues. This growing phenomenon has boosted the importance of the *singles' economy*. For example, single consumers may go to the cinema, KTV (karaoke), or to a restaurant alone. Places that offer solo seats and let them be part of a crowd without standing out will naturally be their first choice. Also, smaller apartments and tiny appliances for solo living are becoming popular with this group. It is interesting to notice that during the 2017 11.11 Shopping Festival,[1]

---

[1] The 11.11 Shopping Festival is China's Black Friday. The festival was first launched by Alibaba in 2009. The festival is a huge sales and entertainment event that is known by a variety of names such as the Double 11 Shopping festival, the Singles' Day Countdown Gala, the Double 11 Countdown Gala, and so on.

purchases of mini appliances rose by 92 percent and *one person use* sales went up by 190 percent. Also, sales of pet supplies and accessories went up 239 percent as single people sought companionship.

Young Males

Another emerging consumption force are young males, especially the post-1995 generation. Unlike their grandfathers and fathers, they are more conscious about their personal image and believe that a tidy appearance is essential for job interviews and dating. As a result, they are willing to spend more on clothing and fitness. Young Chinese men actually spend an average of 24 minutes a day taking care of their appearance. About 88 percent of male consumers living in first-tier cities regularly check out fitness, fashion, and grooming information online, while 83 percent of those between 18 and 35 years think it is necessary to use skincare products and health supplements. A remarkable increase in male grooming products has been noticed, and the total consumption volume for male consumers is getting close to that of female consumers. Searches for men's cosmetics more than doubled during Alibaba's 2017 Singles' Festival. The sales volume of such products is growing rapidly with the total market volume expected to reach 1.9 billion RMB (290 U.S. dollars) in 2019.

Female Luxury Buyers

Although the luxury goods market is female-dominated worldwide, in China, it is still male-dominated. In the past five years, however, consumption by women has been steadily increasing. JD.com, one of China's leading online shopping platforms, reports that women's luxury market is currently worth 2.5 trillion RMB and is expected to grow to 4.5 trillion by 2019. Luxury products like watches, handbags, and cosmetics are becoming more popular, especially among younger, educated women with high incomes. Affordable luxury brands have also gained popularity and managed to build a reputation for high-quality design with relatively affordable prices. Although women are now more willing to spend on luxury goods, they are still price-sensitive. They do thorough research before buying, they choose carefully and believe that interesting offers and discounts are worth waiting for.

To sum up, Chinese consumers are changing fast. They are trendsetters. They are demanding. They expect a lot. They know their power. They travel, study abroad, buy from overseas brands, and export their expectations far and wide. Whether your business is already serving Chinese customers or intends to do so in the future, it is important to understand how they think and buy. Remember that China's main consumer force is made up of people between 15 and 39 years old. It is the 1980s and 1990s generations that make up the majority of online consumers. Most of them are university students, fresh graduates, young professionals, and young parents. They prioritize quality and value over low prices.

Note that:

- over 60 percent of Taobao shoppers belong to the 25–35 years age group,
- over 70 percent come from urban areas and have average monthly revenues of RMB 5,000,
- 30 percent are students,
- 18 percent are white-collar workers,
- 16 percent are self-employed,
- 12 percent are professional technicians, and
- 58 percent of the Internet users are women (they used to represent only 20 percent of the total number of users 15 years ago).

Most offline consumption comes from first- and second-tier cities and other urban areas with high per capita income. On the other hand, when it comes to online consumption, second- and third-tier cities account for an increasingly big share. Although consumers from second-tier cities earn nearly as much as those in first-tier cities, they have fewer options for offline shopping, so they tend to purchase online to fill this gap. Also, compared to first-tier cities, consumers from second-tier cities have more free time to spend shopping online, which translates into greater opportunities for online retailers in these emerging niches. Consumers above 60 years of age also make up 11.2 percent of online consumers. They have more money and time at their disposal after retirement and are a rapidly growing segment of the Chinese population.

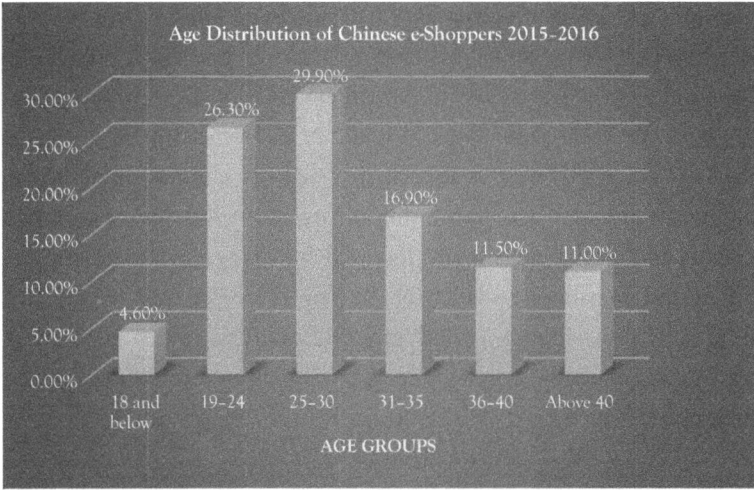

Age Distribution of Chinese e-Shoppers 2015-2016

Source: Fung Business Intelligence Report, 2016.

Number of online shoppers in China 2006–2017

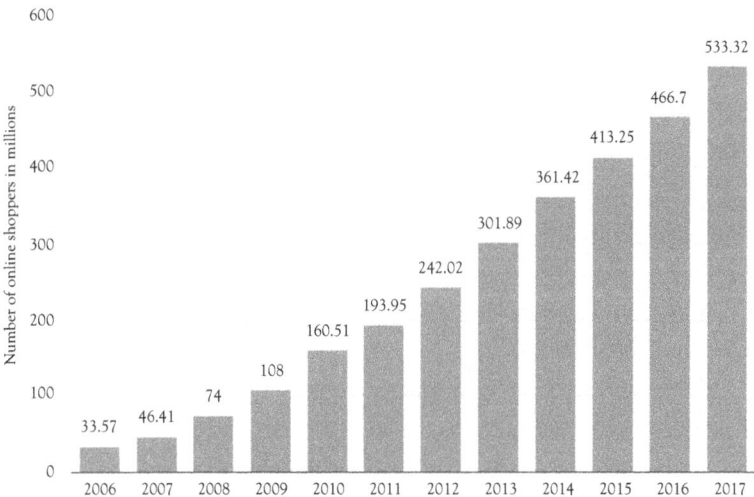

Infographic courtesy of *China Internet Watch*

What Are They Buying?

The latest data from the national Bureau of Statistics shows that, in the first half of 2017, consumption not only accounted for 65 percent of

China's economic growth, but also made up 58 percent of the total GDP. Retail sales have grown at double-digit rates for years, and online sales specifically have increased from 3.8 trillion RMB in 2016 to 5.6 trillion RMB in 2017. Brick-and-mortar vendors experienced huge growth in the sales volume as well. It is clear that Chinese consumers are buying more. The question is: what are they buying and how? Robust economic growth and wealth are usually followed by change in purchasing priorities and consumption behavior. Indeed, there has been a clear shift from daily necessities to a wider group of products, which is accompanied by a remarkable trend toward guilt-free consumption of expensive premium products.

Hi-Tech and Digital

Young Chinese consumers are much more tech-savvy than previous generations. They pay attention to trends and look for the latest tech products and newest models to satisfy their needs for fashion and practicality. A third of Chinese consumers own home or wearable tech products. Purchases of wearable devices and smart household products increased by 22 percent and 20 percent, respectively, in 2017. In terms of high-tech products, virtual reality (VR) is another market with a huge potential. Key domestic digital firms like Tencent and Alibaba will continue to invest heavily in VR in the coming years. VR is already integrated into a variety of industries in China. Retail sales of imaging devices such as VR devices and drones have grown from 650 million RMB in 2016 to 1.6 billion RMB in 2017.

Companies seeking e-commerce opportunities will have to tailor their strategies to account for the special needs and unmet demands of the modern consumer. Brands that will be able to meet the needs of Chinese consumers for better quality and service, will be the winners in an increasingly competitive environment. E-tail will develop rapidly across all product categories through 2018, but the growth potential will vary by product category. Some products are gaining popularity, and they will more than double. One such example is digital cameras. Back in 2010, fewer than 15 percent of the e-shoppers bought cameras online. This number is about to reach 48 percent in 2018, given that a significant number of consumers claim that a digital camera is included in the list of the next three items they plan to purchase online.

Some categories will still enjoy further growth as consumers transfer a larger proportion of their spending from physical stores to e-commerce sites. The casual wear category is also experiencing a significant growth. Apart from casual wear, the categories that are growing faster in terms of online sales are travel, consumer electronics, and cosmetics. In skincare and cosmetics alone, online sales have exceeded combined sales in the United States, the United Kingdom, and Japan to reach over 18 percent of the total retail sales in China. This growth is expected to remain in the double digits, at least for the next five years.

Before entering the Chinese e-commerce sphere, it is important that you have a very clear idea of what your target consumer group wants, what product and service value they expect, and how standards are different from the market(s) your company is used to working in. There are numerous cases of large companies with a successful sales record in Western countries that neglected to adapt to the requirements of the Chinese market, and in the end, failed, eBay being only one famous example among many. A wide variety of products are being made available every day in the Chinese online marketplace. 3C products are the most popular categories for e-commerce in terms of spending in China. The six highest growth categories include fashion, cosmetics, 3C, home appliances, daily necessities, food, and baby products.

The top three product categories for e-shopping that account for 70 percent of all online purchases are (1) apparel, (2) leisure and education, and (3) household products. They are followed by transportation and communications and personal items and health care. Organic products and premium-quality fresh food are also currently in high demand. A category of consumers are still reluctant to shop online for four significant reasons: (1) lack of physical contact with the product, (2) concern about after-sales service, (3) too complicated online payment system, and (4) not owning a debit or credit card. It is important to mention though that the number of online users who decide to buy online has increased dramatically over the past five years, thanks to the creation of sophisticated online platforms, detailed ranking and review systems, and user-friendly payment methods.

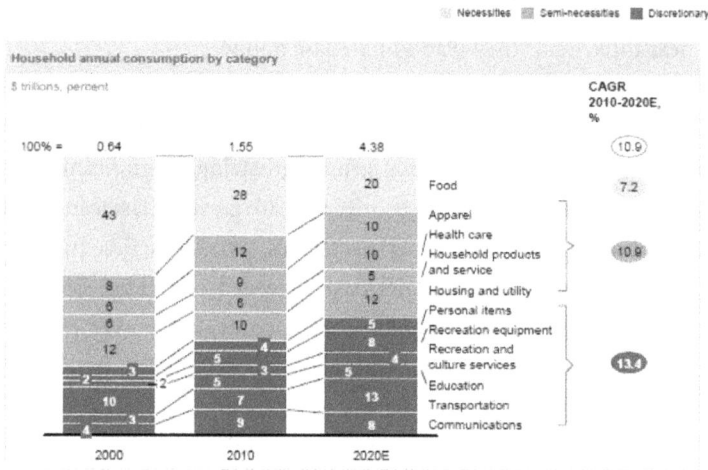

Source: McKinsey China Insights, Macroeconomic Model Update.

Health and Wellness

Chinese people are about to develop a new attitude when it comes to health and well-being. This is not only reflected in shopping trends for daily life necessities such as food and clothing, but also in the new level of consciousness they are about to develop about their overall physical health. China has experienced a number of food safety scandals since 2006. These incidents have involved fake food items, improper use of ingredients, unsafe additives, unhealthy production, and food-processing methods and contaminations. The food products affected have included meat, cooking oil, eggs, noodles, tofu, tapioca, with the most serious being the 2008 milk scandal, including baby formula. As a result, Chinese consumers have grown particularly suspicious when it comes to food quality and product safety. They trust overseas suppliers more and prefer to buy items online or directly from foreign sources when possible. Chinese parents have shown distrust in baby formula and milk products made in China and prefer to buy imported milk powder from the United States and Australia or from Hong Kong and Macau. On the other hand, the booming number of senior citizens adds to the high demand for health supplements and products. An increasingly common gesture is to offer health supplements as gifts to parents and grandparents on special occasions such as birthdays, family celebrations, and festivals. Growing health concerns have also boosted sales of smart devices like watches that count steps or measure heart rate and electronic scales that calculate muscle and body fat. Searches for fitness equipment more than doubled during the 2017 Singles' Festival.

Pollution problems in first-tier cities have also contributed to Chinese consumers pursuing healthier, greener lifestyles. Less labor-intensive work and more personal time also mean that people are more concerned about fitness and well-being than ever before. The number of people pursuing fitness has exceeded 10 million in 2017. This number has maintained an average growth of 10 percent in the past few years. An increasing number of young people, especially the younger ones, hold gym memberships and hire personal trainers for one-on-one coaching sessions. They use fitness apps to create detailed fitness plans, follow instructional videos, and attend fitness courses. This massive trend is also reflected in the popularity of WeRun, a step tracker application within WeChat that includes a ranking system among other features. The number of daily active WeRun users has now reached 115 million with an annual growth of 177 percent.

Entertainment and Tourism

With more disposable income, Chinese consumers are naturally spending more on entertainment. They visit restaurants, cafés, cinemas; they go to KTV (karaoke) more often, and travel more. Travel and entertainment now represent 11 percent of the monthly household spending, which represents twice the amount recorded in 2011. Tourism has witnessed an outstanding growth. Chinese people are traveling more than ever before. National travelers accounted for 4.4 billion in 2016 with an annual growth of 11 percent. Among them, a growing number shows a strong willingness to travel abroad. Outbound travelers hit a record high of 122 million, with a year-on-year growth of 4.5 percent. This segment still holds a huge potential. Chinese travelers are also adopting Western travel habits. Instead of just going sightseeing and shopping, they are more willing to engage in in-depth experiences of local, authentic lifestyle and culture. Custom-tailored travel services are a growing trend. Many are moving from five-star hotels to boutique hotels or AirBnB homestays, while bespoke and VIP tours are also growing in popularity.

Luxury and Premium Products

The impulse to show status with premium products is very strong in China. *You are what you wear* and many also believe that high-quality products improve their lives. Luxury products are a key high-end with an astonishing growth. In 2016 alone, 7.6 million Chinese households were estimated to have purchased luxury goods, each spending an average of 72,000 RMB (approximately 12,000 U.S. dollars) per year. This is twice what households in legacy luxury markets like France and Italy spend on luxury goods. In 2017, the market witnessed an incredible growth reaching a total market size of about 24 billion U.S. dollars. The major reason is that a growing number of fashion-savvy Chinese consumers have started to shop more online, which has contributed to the sales growth. The luxury market is still due to grow in volume and importance. The number of Chinese millionaires is expected to surpass that of any other nation in 2018. By 2021, China is expected to have the most affluent households in the world, while by 2025, the number of Chinese luxury consumers is expected to reach 150 million.

How Are They Buying?

With the expansion of e-commerce and technology, Chinese consumers are gradually decreasing their purchases from brick-and-mortar stores and turn to e-commerce platforms more and more. In China, social media also serve as search engines. One of WeChat's major goals for 2018 is to improve its search function accuracy. With WeChat Search, users can see the engagement between other users and brands, they can access recently published content by their favorite brands, and read comments on their favorite posts, articles, and official accounts. Other major social media platforms like Weibo, Douban, and Zhihu are often used to find product information and user recommendations. Let us now take a look at how Chinese consumers shop online and which are the steps they follow from pre-purchase, through purchase to post-purchase.

Pre-Purchase

Search

Doing online search before purchasing has become common practice in many parts of the world. China is no different. Price, quality, and similar products are compared before consumers decide on which product to buy. In addition to domestic search engines like Baidu and Sougou, Chinese consumers search on e-commerce platforms like Taobao, JD.com, Xiaohongshu, and so on. For niche categories, there are vertical social platforms like qyer.com for travel and Babytree for parenting and childcare products. The search results are updated in real time and customized based on data such as the user's search and browsing history, as well as their location. This process often leads directly to purchases. Recommendations often appear as display ads, and platforms also show product and brand suggestions that, very often, are spot-on. While few Western consumers say they would purchase an item after seeing its ad, a third of Chinese consumers admit they would purchase it after seeing the ad. This type of advertising drives exceptionally high click-through rates and longer visits on the advertised platforms.

Reviews and Peer Recommendations

Chinese consumers check product information and read peer reviews from other customers and professional bloggers, while those following celebrities on social media are likely to buy products they showcase or recommend in their videos. Users take comments and product reviews very seriously. Almost half of them leave reviews and comments about items they bought, whereas Western consumers are less likely to do.

While Purchasing

See Now, Buy Now: Live Demos

The *see now, buy now* function offers a more memorable experience for viewers and customers and leads to more sales conversions. Live streaming has become a hit since 2015 in China, and e-commerce platforms like Tmall developed a live streaming function that allows vendors to showcase their products to potential customers in a more memorable and eye-catching way. These live demos allow viewers to ask questions about a specific product and interact with fellow viewers through comments. Sellers display their products, demonstrate how they can be used, and answer customer questions. If a viewer is interested in a product, they can simply click the item on the screen and purchase it immediately.

Buy What You See!: Social Media Marketing

Users have the possibility to shop directly on social media platforms like Weibo and WeChat. These platforms allow users to embed product links from partnered e-commerce platforms. On WeChat, for example, you can embed direct links to product pages from Taobao.com, JD.com, and so on. Whenever people see something they like on these platforms, they can buy them immediately by simply clicking on the embedded links that are displayed. The *Buy What You See* function takes product placement to the next level, making the path from discovery to purchase as smooth and natural as possible.

Mobile Payments and Immediate Distribution

By speeding up the online purchase system, fast and safe mobile payment options are a key factor behind the increasing popularity of online shopping in China. Alipay and WeChat Pay are the most widely used mobile payment tools, developed by Alibaba and Tencent, respectively. Users can make purchases and complete payments by using their fingerprint or a password to confirm payment. Money is then automatically deducted from their digital wallet or from the bank account they have linked to their digital wallet. In 2017, Alipay introduced more advanced security measures, such as facial recognition, to ensure safety during transactions. Once the payment is completed, express delivery service providers such as SF express, Cainiao, and JD Logistics play a crucial role in timely distribution. Logistics has evolved into a very transparent process, and packages can be monitored online with a tracking number. In first-tier cities, orders can be delivered within 15 minutes of the order being placed.

Post-Purchase

Feedback

After buyers receive the product they purchased, most e-commerce platforms encourage them to rate the product and their overall shopping experience and add comments that will be used as a reference for future buyers with respect to the quality of the product. They also answer questions from prospective buyers about their experience with a similar product. If they feel dissatisfied with the product, buyers often contact the brand's social media account. Customers can submit enquiries or make complaints directly by leaving comments under the seller's most recent posts or by simply sending a direct message. This is usually far more efficient than making phone calls or writing a formal e-mail. Professional bloggers post daily product reviews on social media, sharing their consumer experience and talk about the pros and cons of a particular product and often compare it to competitor products.

Weak Brand Loyalty

Chinese shoppers are far from being loyal to brands. Rather, they are adventurous and open to new brands and products. They are easily attracted by innovative offerings and creative multimedia content. A recent study revealed that about three-fourths of Chinese respondents turned to new brands and products in 2017. At the same time, a growing number of brands are entering China. As a result, this has given way to an even more fragmented market. Existing established brands are, therefore, at risk of losing once-loyal customers.

The Weight of Heavy Spenders

Consumerism is already a phenomenon in China. The more familiar Chinese netizens become with online shopping, the more money they tend to spend. People in Beijing and Shanghai have a disposable personal income (DPI) level of more than 62,000 RMB per year (approximately 18,300 U.S. dollars), while Tianjin and Shenzhen closely follow behind with more than 38,000 RMB per year (approximately 6,000 U.S. dollars) of DPI. Chinese e-shoppers can be divided into four separate consumer segments according to how much of their disposable income they spend online. They range from light spenders to moderate to heavy then to super-heavy.

It is important to notice that 7 percent of online consumers account for 40 percent of the total online spending. These are the super-heavy spenders. They spend more than RMB 10,000 (1,700 U.S. dollars) per year on online shopping. Light spenders spend no more than RMB 1,000 (165 U.S. dollars) per year. They represent 60 percent of total e-shoppers and account for less than 15 percent of the total online spending. The heavy spenders' segment engage in a larger number of transactions and their purchases include a wide range of product categories, whereas light spenders' purchases focus mostly on the apparel category. Super-heavy spenders buy on average 175 items and engage in 50 transactions per year. On the other hand, light spenders buy 22 items on average over the course of 10 transactions per year.

Chinese consumers become increasingly heavy spenders as they accumulate more wealth. A pleasant shopping experience is a major driving force for online spending. Very wealthy shoppers with little e-shopping experience normally spend 60 percent less than experienced middle-class shoppers. Over 70 percent of the super-heavy spenders come from the middle and affluent classes and have been shopping online for more than six years. It normally takes affluent e-shoppers four to six years to become super-heavy spenders.

Although bargain hunting is an essential part of the whole online shopping adventure for them, these consumers are increasingly looking beyond discounted products. They actively look for branded, unique, premium-quality products that are often not available offline. They tend to be emotionally attached to online shopping, and they value better customer service, convenience, speed, and the fun part of shopping online. E-shopping has become more of a pastime, not to say a hobby, for them. Another characteristic of this group is that they are very likely to go shopping online without having any specific product in mind. Taking into consideration their greater propensity to make an unplanned purchase in order to fulfill their emotional needs, this growing segment will soon become the target group of many brands. Also, considering the strong emotional ties that Chinese consumers have with shopping, it is essential to attract them with unique value propositions that go beyond mere low prices. In a few words, the best way to attract super-heavy spenders is to make them feel special by focusing on quality and customer service. Meeting the emotional needs of super-heavy spenders will be the key to brands' future success in the Chinese e-merging market. Companies can achieve this by offering customers a fun shopping experience or by giving them the feeling that they are learning something through the whole process.

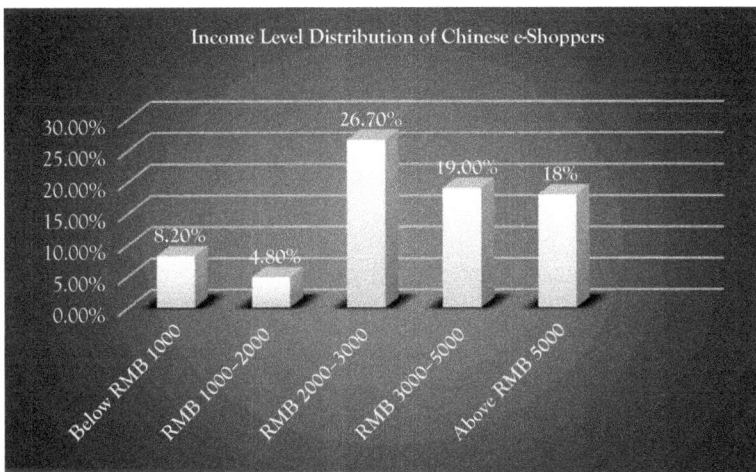

Source: China's National Bureau of Statistics, 2017, EUSME.

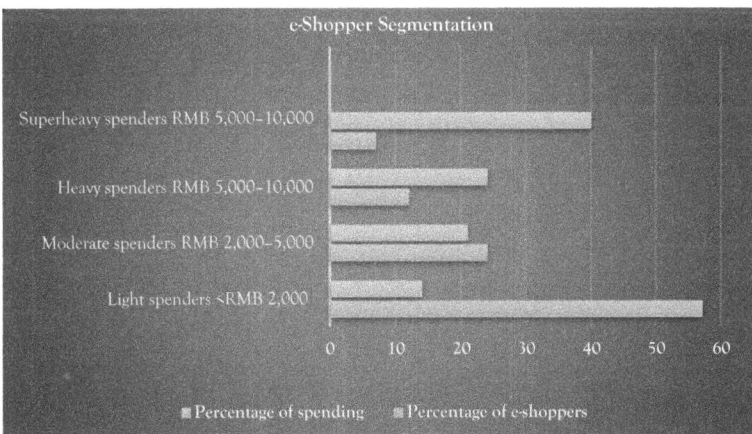

Source: China's National Bureau of Statistics, 2016–2017, EUSME.

What Do They Value Most?

Basic Expectations of Chinese Online Consumers

The following checklist is crucial when it comes to meeting the basic consumer needs and expectations in China:

- Products—be it cheap or very high-end products—sold online should be cheaper than the ones sold in traditional retail stores.
- A strong value proposition is very important if you do not want to end up competing solely on price.
- Make sure you know your target customers and try your best to deliver unmatched value, quality, and service.
- Payment methods offered to customers should be simple and fast. The required fields should typically be limited to contact, address, and payment details.
- Same- or next-day delivery is expected in first-tier cities like Shanghai and Beijing, while delivery in second-, third-, and fourth-tier cities is normally expected within two to three business days.

Growth by Region

Thanks to the Chinese government's efforts to improve the country's telecommunications infrastructure and make the Internet accessible to the largest possible number of households, Internet access is pretty affordable and accessible to approximately 90 percent of the Chinese population. Broadband Internet monthly fees are no more than 10 U.S. dollars, while in India, broadband Internet costs 30 U.S. dollars per month and in Brazil 27 U.S. dollars. China gained on average 74 to 88 million Internet users each year since 2006, that is, a volume larger than the entire population of France. Throughout these years, consumers moved from having a limited familiarity with online shopping to a relatively high level of adaptation.

Another important factor that has benefited the e-tail industry is the low cost of shipping which is 1 U.S. dollar on average for a parcel weighing 1 kg, while the same parcel in the United States would cost 6 U.S. dollars.

Among the 334 cities in China, 314 are inland cities of various sizes. They generate 65 percent of China's GDP. By the end of 2010, there were about 120 million middle- and higher-class households with annual disposable income exceeding RMB 50,000 (8,200 U.S. dollars) in China. About 88 million more are expected to emerge in the next 10 years. Among them, 77 percent will come from inland cities. As market growth slows in the country's developed coastal areas, the expanding middle-class households in inland cities look more attractive and are of greater significance to a company's success. Coastal cities in China currently represent 47 percent of the total online shopping value with the top regions being Shanghai, Beijing, Guangdong, Zhejiang, and Jiangsu.

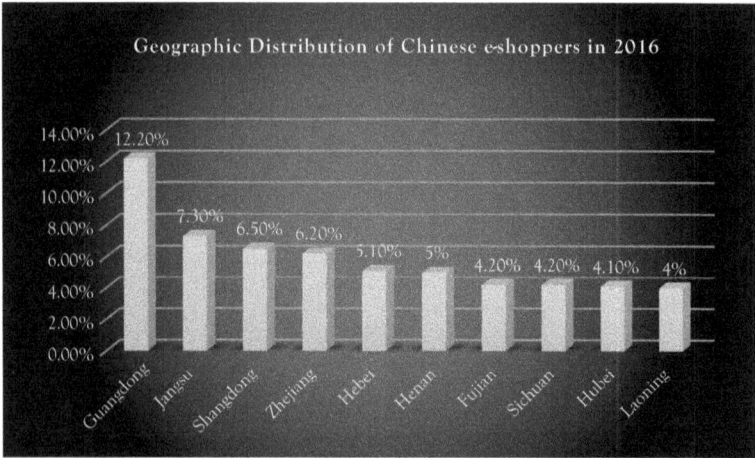

Geographic Distribution of Chinese e-shoppers in 2016

Guangdong 12.20%, Jiangsu 7.30%, Shangdong 6.50%, Zhejiang 6.20%, Hebei 5.10%, Henan 5%, Fujian 4.20%, Sichuan 4.20%, Hubei 4.10%, Laoning 4%

Source: Fung Business Intelligence Report, 2016.

How to Market Your Products and Services Online

The question of how to market your products to Chinese consumers is one that is debated endlessly by foreign companies seeking to profit from the tremendous potential of the Chinese market. It is difficult to conduct serious marketing research in China. Often, the difficulty in gaining access to and unreliability of information might expose corporate decisions to additional risks. Although East–West cultural differences remain a challenge to foreign companies carrying out marketing in China, those companies that make an effort to understand such differences and integrate them into their marketing and sales strategy stand a far greater chance of succeeding in the Chinese market. Businesses with a patient, flexible, and *listening* marketing and sales approach will be able to succeed in China.

Overcoming Early Challenges

To overcome the initial challenges, a China market entry strategy involving different stages is highly recommended, starting with the central issue of what kind of business activities are to be pursued by the company in China. As a next step, the geographical orientation and form of investment need to be determined. Questions might include whether a production facility will be established or whether efforts will be merely focused on marketing and sales, or whether a combination of these strategies serves better the needs of the company.

The types of websites Chinese consumers choose for their online shopping differ greatly from those in other countries. Less than 20 percent of e-shoppers visit official brand or manufacturer websites as opposed to 60 percent in the United States, Japan, and the European Union. What happens currently is that the Chinese website versions of most foreign brands are usually direct translations of their Western sites, which are little or not at all customized for the Chinese market. Such companies have failed or simply neglected to create customized platforms to give customers a sense of familiarity and encourage them to visit more frequently. The distinctive behavior and special needs of Chinese buyers should be taken into account by any company that is seriously considering to enter the Chinese e-commerce market. Your company's homepage is the place to begin.

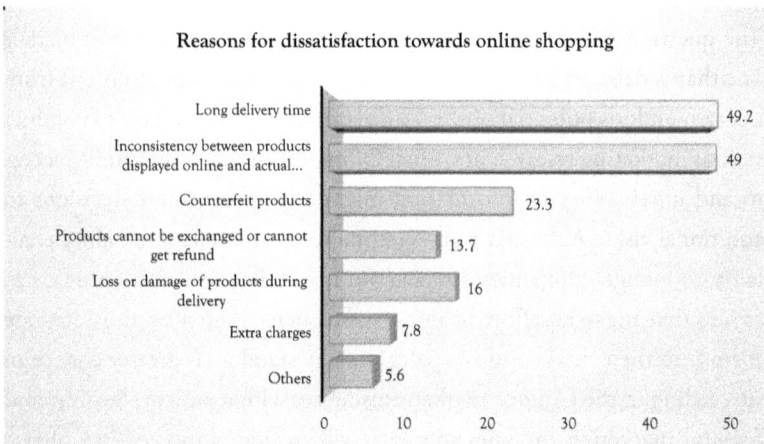

Reasons for dissatisfaction towards online shopping

Category	Value
Long delivery time	49.2
Inconsistency between products displayed online and actual...	49
Counterfeit products	23.3
Products cannot be exchanged or cannot get refund	13.7
Loss or damage of products during delivery	16
Extra charges	7.8
Others	5.6

Another challenge to e-commerce is a low level of trust in a consumer population that is wary of inferior quality or fake goods. Chinese consumers are probably the most social compared to any other country when it comes to online shopping. One reason behind this active online social behavior when it comes to shopping is an underlying distrust of products sold online and the impossibility to test the real quality of the offerings. Relying on recommendations or reviews from members of their social network helps alleviate some of the distrust consumers tend to have of online merchants. Another thing to bear in mind is that trust in online information sources like social networking sites, blogs, or review sites is much higher than trust in offline sources such as TV or printed ads.

Chinese Social Media Platforms: How to Work with Them to Increase Profitability

The very essence of Chinese mentality is based on *guanxi*. From the very beginning of Chinese civilization, people followed a precise set of rules and ways of doing things. Peoples' lives were determined by customs, traditional beliefs, and social laws. Every single aspect of their lives was set by precedent, and this included the place where they lived, the clothes they wore, their profession, their education, the person they married, and how they related to other people. All these beliefs and social practices have shaped the foundations of the Chinese mindset up to the present day. It is no wonder that, in such a society, the famous adage "It's not what you know, it's who you know" evolved into a mantra, especially in the context of social and business relations. In other words, it is generally not a person's intelligence, hardworking qualities, knowledge, or merit that determines their success in life, society, and business, but it is rather *guanxi*, the personal connections they have, and the way they use them to achieve their aims. It is important to know that all efforts made by foreigners to get by in China without developing and nurturing *guanxi* will be doomed to failure. China being a very bureaucratic country, you will very likely need *guanxi* to skip some very time-consuming procedures or at least to make things work faster for your business. Because these relations are hard to build and require time, especially for foreigners, an alternative widespread method you can use to escape red tape or get things done faster is the *hong bao*, which means *red envelope*. Chinese people use to put money in a red envelope and give it to a person in exchange for a service that would otherwise be too hard or time-consuming to get.

Social media are not only a new way of developing one's *guanxi* network and professional connections in China, but most importantly, a key uniting factor in this chaotic digital market. Social media are a very powerful customer relationship management tool for both micro and macro businesses. Social media also play a crucial role in strategies used not only by SMEs, but by leading industry players as well. With the astonishing growth of mobile technology in recent years, more and more people are using social media to connect with each other, to share their experiences, thoughts, and achievements, to obtain information and of course … to buy, buy, buy. Because of this, Chinese social media can work as an important entry point to the Chinese market. To do so, a brand's social media account should be thought of and operate pretty much like a business branch. Social media are becoming an increasingly important lead-generation channel, and failing to use it effectively will cost you money. Therefore, it is not uncommon for brands to have a lot more consumer interactions on their WeChat account than on their actual website. However, having a minimal website presence is still required for the sake of credibility, online brand image, and control of your product labels.

Differences and Similarities in Social Media Usage: China Versus the West

The main similarity between Chinese and Western social media users is that they both use social media primarily for instant messaging and as a way to catch up on the latest news and entertainment. For Chinese users, on top of everything else, social media are also an e-commerce channel where they look for deals, discounts, and where they hold lucky draws. To check out the latest news and trends and look for purchase recommendations, they follow the accounts of celebrities and influencers. They then make purchases on social media through integrated online stores.

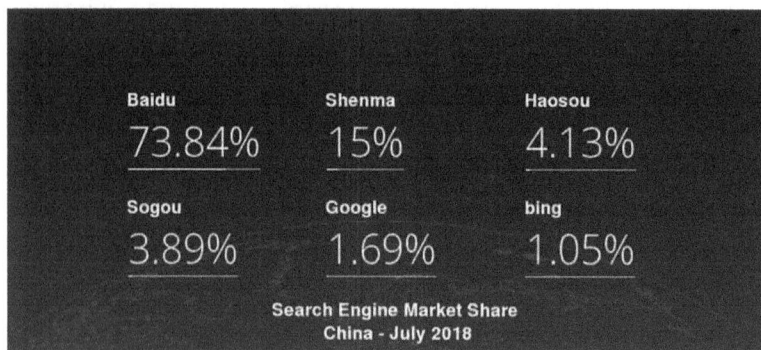

Baidu	Shenma	Haosou
73.84%	15%	4.13%
Sogou	Google	bing
3.89%	1.69%	1.05%

Search Engine Market Share
China - July 2018

The Chinese Social Media Landscape

The Chinese digital landscape is fragmented. Major platforms like WeChat, Weibo, Baidu, and Taobao dominate the digital arena. Platforms are categorized by function (live streaming, blogging, image sharing, etc.) or cater to specific niche audiences such as students, professionals, music fans, artists, and so on. In the next section, you can find a description of the key steps you will need to follow for a successful—and hopefully profitable—use of the leading Chinese social media platforms:

Baidu

Baidu is the Google of China. It offers additional services such as *Baidu Tieba*, which is a discussion forum and Baidu Zhidao; literally meaning *Baidu Knows*. Baidu Zhidao is a question and answer website. The following key points will help your company make an effective use of Baidu:

- *Present content in a way that follows key search terms.* Online users look for a product using entries such as *fashionable brand T-shirt*, or *organic meat in Shanghai*. For this reason, you should consider local search engine optimization services so that your products will pop up in search results.
- *Get a localized microsite.* I urge you to get a localized microsite built from scratch in accordance with Chinese browser habits and user experience (UX) interaction guidelines. If your online marketing strategy is limited to appending webpages with content in Chinese to a website hosted in your home country, you can be certain that it will not work. Pages will simply not be visible on Chinese search engines.
- *Make sure your website is fully accessible within China.* Ideally, your website should be hosted within the Chinese government firewall. If not, loading times are likely to be slow to a point where your website becomes practically inaccessible. An ICP (Internet content provider) license is required for all business websites in China. Please refer to the section *Selling Through a Standalone Website Inside China* for further details on the requirements and procedures when applying for such a license.
- *Be aware of differences in search processes.* Due to the complexity of the Chinese language, paid searches differ from those used in the United States and other Western countries. As a result, the bidding of keywords and structure of accounts are affected. For instance, on Baidu, *phrase match* functions more like *modified broad search*, and *broad match* captures a lot more queries because of the complex structure of the Chinese language.
- *Keep text and pages simple to achieve better SEO results.* Baidu's web crawling spider is less powerful than Google bot. As a

consequence, it crawls no deeper than three levels. For this reason, companies should place important information at the top of each webpage and limit their keyword density percentage to between 6 and 10 percent.

Weibo

Weibo literally means *microblog* and is the Chinese equivalent of Twitter. It is available through various platforms, but the leading ones are Sina Weibo and Tencent Weibo. Some common features Weibo shares with Twitter include the possibility of posting 140-character long comments, pictures, and videos. They differ in terms of user activity though. The main difference being that, while most Twitter postings are related to news, Weibo users' comments focus on topics related to entertainment. Another major difference is that Sina Weibo is particularly popular among urban dwellers. Most Weibo users are university students and young professionals, whereas the majority of Tencent users come from rural parts of the country.

Renren and Qzone

Renren—along with Qzone—is considered to be the Chinese Facebook. Qzone and QQ users are typically young people below the age of 18 years. As they grow older, they tend to move to Renren, which is mainly used by young adults. Although Tencent's Qzone may count a larger number of users than Renren, it has been criticized as being heavily populated by rural and teenage users who use nicknames instead of real identities. Renren users are generally more transparent.

Youku

Youku is the Chinese equivalent of YouTube. There are, however, substantial differences between them. YouTube videos are user-generated, whereas the majority of Youku's content is syndicated. Youku mainly features longer videos, rather than short music videos like YouTube. It offers excellent opportunities as a forum for reaching potential customers. You can create a professional video of your product or service and upload it there, or hire a Chinese spokesperson to post regular video reviews of your products on Youku as part of your marketing strategy.

Key Online Marketing Strategies

Since its inception, Chinese society has been based on *connections*, what Chinese people famously call *guanxi*, a term that has been already explained. Networking plays a major role in their everyday life. A large number of networking websites have emerged over the last couple of years. These online social networks have given *guanxi* a new form. Chinese social networking sites can be very profitable if used in a smart way. About 80 percent of the Chinese Internet users closely follow commercial information posted on social networking websites. Over 50 percent of these users consider their friends' comments as reliable references on which they base their own purchasing decisions. Around 38 percent share their shopping experience by posting links of their favorite products and brands, while 25 percent would complain on social media sites about an unpleasant shopping experience they had.

SMM (social media marketing) tools are an essential part of any digital marketing strategy and will help you establish better communication with your existing or potential customers. It is a very cost-saving way of building your brand's reputation in China and driving more traffic to your website, be it an independent website or your Taobao or Tmall storefront. Effective social media marketing campaigns, well combined with offline marketing, will help build long-term relationships with your customers by engaging them in the promotion of your products and services.

The social media platforms listed earlier are a must for every international company operating in the Chinese online marketplace. I recommend that you open a corporate and personal account with at least five of them. Make sure you use Q-zone, Tencent Weibo, and Sina Weibo. Recent research on social networking behavior revealed that more than 90 percent of the total population of Chinese Internet users visited a social media platform in the previous three months. About 95 percent of the Internet users who live in the country's largest cities own at least one social media account. Another characteristic of social media users is their tendency to be very active. Chinese netizens spend an average of

48 minutes per day on social media websites, compared to an average of 10 minutes in Japan and 36 in the United States. However, not all users behave in the same way. Motivation and behavior vary between groups. Six different user profiles have been identified:

- *Social media enthusiasts* spend a large amount of their spare time building online friendship networks. They represent 35 percent of the total population of social media users in China.
- *Reposters* represent 42 percent of users. Their activity consists in actively reposting popular comments coming from other sources. Although the material they post is not original, they usually attract large numbers of followers.
- *Readers* read content posted by others, but they are generally passive. They account for 55 percent of users.
- *Opinionated users* represent 14 percent of social media users. They express their own—usually strong—opinions, and generally, have a large number of followers.
- *QQ spillovers* access social media sites through Tencent's instant messaging application. Although they represent 21 percent of the social media users, their participation is limited.
- *Inactives* are registered users to social media sites, but they seldom participate in any of them.

More than 80 percent of the entire user population in China is active on more than one social site. Despite the fact that exact numbers of users cannot be established—partly because of issues related to virtual or fake users—it is clear that Qzone along with Tencent Weibo and Sina Weibo are by far the most popular social sites.

The Big Two: Wechat and Sina Weibo

Wechat (微信)

Wechat, known in Chinese as Weixin (微信), started as a mobile instant messaging application, but has grown to include features such as Moments, official accounts, and WeChat Pay. WeChat is the most widely used application in China. For the sake of clarity, the word *WeChat* in this book refers to the Chinese version of the app by its English name, not to the international version, which is different from the Chinese one.

Sina Weibo (新浪微博)

Weibo is China's largest microblogging platform. It can be described as a combination of Facebook and Twitter. It is a fast-flowing information source, trend-spotter, and trendsetter. Back in 2010, there were many microblogging platforms in China, created by Sina, Sohu, Tencent, and NetEase. During that time, Sina Weibo and Tencent Weibo were the leading microblogging giants that dominated the market. Sina was the first to build a microblogging service in China. Thanks to its first-mover advantage, the company was able to get many celebrities to open accounts on their platform, thus exploding the number of users in just one year. Tencent launched its own microblogging site a year later, as a defense move against Sina Weibo. By 2012, Tencent Weibo's user base had reached 540 million, surpassing Sina Weibo's 503 million user base. Sina Weibo had achieved a spectacular popularity since its launch, but began losing momentum in 2012, when discussions began about the death of Weibo. Social analysts had then pointed out various possible causes for Weibo's slowdown, but the main reasons were the rise of WeChat and the government's media crackdown.

Since 2012, the government increased its control and censorship of mass media, including Sina Weibo. As the platform enables people to express their opinions and make them public, debate around controversial issues can spread quickly. The government has introduced measures to tamp down online debate and increase its control of microblogging platforms by requiring real-name registration, as well as by launching anti-rumor campaigns. On top of that, WeChat was launched in 2011 and expanded very rapidly. As a result, many Weibo users began to spend more time on WeChat in the years following its launch. WeChat offers a more closed setup, and its messaging and social networking functions provided an additional way for users to connect and interact. Weibo experienced a 40 percent decline in active users in 2012, and a significant drop of 56 million registered accounts in 2014. However, it is now much more than what it was back then. Sina implemented new strategies in order to rebuild their user base. For example, they began to tap into users from younger age groups as well as users in lower-tier cities. Starting in 2013, they launched a pre-installed app, and in 2014, they initiated a campaign to sponsor bloggers and KOLs (key opinion leaders) to create content.

Most importantly, the huge popularity of live streaming and short videos have played a key role in Weibo's renaissance. In 2013, Weibo partnered with Miaopai, a leading video-sharing app, and Yizhibo, a popular live-streaming app. Users can now access both of them via Weibo. As a result, many celebrities and KOLs have relocated to Weibo, and as a result, their fans are following them there. Monthly active users had a net 70 million year-on-year growth and reached 411 million in the first quarter of 2018, while daily active users had a net addition of approximately 30 million users year-on-year to reach 184 million in March 2018.[2]

You can easily find the day's most discussed topics on Weibo and use them as part of your marketing strategy. Posts can include text, images, articles, external links, audios, and videos. Weibo users can follow other accounts, comment, repost, and like articles and posts. However, while comments and updates are public, messages are private.

What Is WeChat?

WeChat—known in China as Weixin—started in 2011 as a free instant messaging application by Tencent. It grew very fast and added functions.

---

[2] China Internet Watch, 2018.

Inside China, it is used to do everything from ordering food and paying bills to buying international flight tickets. After Weixin's massive success, an international version was developed: WeChat. This version maintains some of the same functions, but the two systems use different server bases. For the sake of simplicity, the term WeChat is used for the easier understanding of English speakers, but it normally refers to Weixin as used in China. Chinese netizens rely heavily on WeChat.

By the end of 2017, Weixin and WeChat together had 980 million monthly active users. This number was up 15.8 percent compared to 2016. As of September 2017, an average of 902 million users have logged in daily, which represents an annual growth of 17 percent. Over half of the Chinese netizens spend more than 90 minutes per day on WeChat. The app is widely used for work by 90 percent of its users.

Weixin Versus WeChat International Version

Many people think that WeChat and Weixin are the same, and that Weixin is only the Chinese name for WeChat. This is part of the story. This book focuses on how to use WeChat (Weixin), the China-based version of WeChat. Again, it is for the sake of clarity that it is referred to by its English name: WeChat.

Weixin is the version for users within China, while WeChat's international version is designed for users outside of China. They do not belong to the same system of servers. Though they have similar interfaces and many common features, they differ in several and significant ways. Marketers seeking customers in Mainland China need to be aware of these differences, or they may end up targeting the wrong audience. As already mentioned, Weixin and WeChat target different user groups in different regions. Weixin operates in Mainland China, while WeChat's international version serves overseas users. When users download the app, the version is determined by the phone number used during the first login. Therefore, you get Weixin from the China-based app store if your phone number and phone location are based in China and if your phone's user interface is in Chinese. Overseas users get the international version of WeChat. In the same fashion, official WeChat accounts differ from Weixin official accounts. Because the Chinese and international versions use different servers, official account data is stored in different places.

Weixin users are not able to search for or subscribe to official accounts registered on the international version. They cannot participate in campaigns or promotions run by international official accounts due to strict web regulations in Mainland China. However, users of the international version can search for official Weixin accounts and participate in their campaigns. Until recently, Weixin official accounts were not permitted for companies outside of Mainland China. However, starting from 2018, businesses in Hong Kong, Macao, Taiwan, Korea, and Japan can now set up official accounts that will be visible on the app within the mainland.

Another major difference lies in the wallet functions for the two versions. For example, China-based users can pay for a wide range of services and products using their Weixin wallet, but these options are not available to users of the international version. So far, international users have more limited wallet functions except in South Africa. Foreigners living in Mainland China, Taiwan, Macao, and Hong Kong can activate WeChat Pay accounts and link them to overseas credit cards. As regions outside of China use different currencies and are governed by different financial regulations, WeChat and Weixin depend on different third-party payment systems. Other features also differ slightly between the two versions. For those targeting the mainland users, they need to register an official account on Weixin—not the international version—and go through the required procedures for activation and verification. The following section details how to do that.

WeChat's Working Model

As the most used app and most popular social media platform in China, WeChat has developed a unique working model that covers everything from social networking to marketing, sales, and CRM, with convenience and integration at its core.

Social Networking and Daily Necessities

WeChat being fundamentally a social networking app with instant messaging as its core function, users can send messages to their contacts and chat groups or make audio and video calls. WeChat also offers a popular social networking feature, which is called *Moments* in English, but in actuality is

- Instant messaging
- Moments
- Booking services
- Payment services

- Targeted messaging
- Loyalty programs
- Member management

Social and daily necessities

CRM

Sales

Marketing

- WeChat wallet
- WeChat pay
- WeChat stores

- Advertising
- Articles
- Campaigns
- KOLs

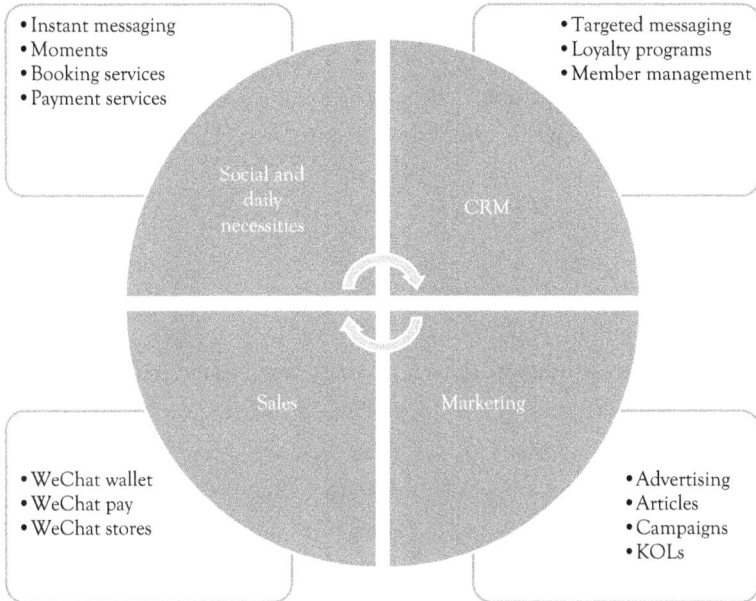

called *Friends' Circle* in Chinese. Users can update their status, share content, and post links to external websites. Their contacts can like and post comments below these posts, which makes the Moments page pretty much like Facebook's wall and news feed. In terms of daily necessities, WeChat can also be used to pay utility bills, hire a taxi, book train tickets, and access a wide variety of city-based medical, housing, and transportation services.

Marketing and Advertising

Given WeChat's growing popularity in China, it can be an excellent tool for marketing and advertising. In 2012, WeChat launched the Official Accounts function. Official accounts allow enterprises, organizations, celebrities, and media to broadcast messages or articles to their followers. It is an effective and low-cost way to promote their brand and connect with individual users, thus improving customer loyalty. Fans and regular users receive updates and can have direct conversations with these brands. WeChat aims to integrate advertising into UX with its major ad types displayed in Moments and WeChat articles. The two types of ads differ from each other in their format, pricing model, and minimum spending. It is important to understand that WeChat is not a strategy. It is a channel. It is only worth the consumer value proposal you build for it. Therefore, it is essential that you build a WeChat user journey that will be as personal as possible. How? By understanding who your followers are, what they care about the most, and how you can meet their unmet needs.

Sales

Alipay and WeChat Pay have revolutionized the payment habits of Chinese consumers, and together account for about 90 percent of China's mobile payment industry. Driven by these two mobile payment giants, China is about to transform from a heavily cash-based society to a largely cashless one. Every user has a WeChat Wallet, which they usually link to WeChat account to transfer money or complete other transactions. WeChat Wallet allows all sorts of transactions; from booking theater tickets to paying utility bills and transferring money to friends' accounts, completing offline payments, or giving virtual monetary gifts, such as red envelopes that are traditionally offered to relatives and friends during the Chinese New Year celebration. WeChat was, in fact, the first to establish the tradition of virtual red packets. WeChat also facilitates offline transactions by allowing brands to set up their own WeChat Pay account. This allows buyers to pay vendors using their WeChat Wallet simply by scanning a QR code or showing their unique payment code. To enable users to go through the entire purchase process without exiting from their application, WeChat supports WeChat stores that have set up official accounts with the app.

Customer Relationship Management

As a semi-closed platform, WeChat is good for customer relationship management (CRM), as it allows more intimate messaging between brands and customers. However, CRM on WeChat is much more than that. In addition to one-on-one messaging, WeChat offers other CRM features like user demographics analysis for brands to develop a more in-depth understanding of their followers, template messages as service notifications, and a custom menu bar that directs users to different services provided by the brand or helps them find the information they are looking for quickly. More sophisticated CRM systems, like chatbots, can be integrated into WeChat to deal with simple enquiries, digital forms, and other advanced functions like food ordering services, hotel or restaurant booking, as well as location-based navigation.

WeChat's Strongest Point: Convenience and Integration

The combination of all aforementioned aspects has made WeChat very convenient to use. People have the possibility to get anything done within WeChat. In early 2017, Tencent officially released its WeChat Mini Program platform. Mini programs are cloud-based embedded apps within WeChat. This means that users will not have to install extra applications from other parties as they currently do. Most importantly, mini programs do not take up precious phone memory and can store user data in WeChat's servers that are linked to the users' accounts.

This way, WeChat aims to allow users to perform all their mobile activities within their platform, without needing additional apps. In the future, people may only need WeChat installed on their smartphone. WeChat has evolved into much more that the instant messaging app it was a couple of years ago. In addition to social networking, it has strengthened its position in marketing, advertising, e-commerce, and mobile payments. Expanding in all these areas has enabled the app to gradually fulfill its ambition to be the ultimate operating system for life in China.

How to Market on WeChat

Official Accounts

Official accounts are the most important tool for brand marketing and advertising. They provide an effective channel for government, businesses, media, industry leaders, and famous people to promote themselves or their brands to millions of users. In early 2017, there were approximately 3.5 million monthly active official accounts and 797 million monthly active subscribers, representing an annual growth of 14 percent. According to Stephen Wang, WeChat's User Growth and Engagement Director, the articles read monthly by the average user equal a novel.

The Three Main Types of Official Accounts

To start marketing on WeChat, the first step is to open an official account for your brand. Currently, there are three main types of official accounts:

- Subscription Accounts
- Service Accounts
- Corporate Accounts

Each of these accounts meets different marketing needs.

Subscription Accounts

Subscription accounts, designed primarily for updates and communication, are the most basic type of official accounts. Their major advantage is that they allow account holders to publish articles or send messages once a day. They can publish up to eight articles each time. This makes them a good choice for media and businesses that are heavily content-based and post content frequently. Bloggers and famous individuals can only open subscription accounts.

Such accounts are listed under the *Subscriptions* folder on the home page. Users do not receive notifications when new articles or messages are published to minimize disturbance for those who follow several accounts. A red dot appears in the top-right corner of the account's avatar, indicating an unread message. Users have to click into the folder to check out the latest updates. In the folder, all the accounts the user has subscribed to are displayed according to their last update time.

Service Accounts

This type of accounts offer more advanced features for businesses and organizations. For example, their CRM system is more complex because it integrates booking services, WeChat-affiliated stores, and loyalty programs. Service accounts support more advanced features, such as WeChat Pay, location-based services, and speech–text conversion. Service accounts focus more on customer service and sales, so they only allow account holders to publish four times a month, each time up to eight articles. Unlike subscription accounts, service accounts appear on the chat list on the homepage. Users receive a notification once messages or articles are published, like when they receive messages from their contacts. This ensures greater visibility and a feeling of familiarity. All these elements make service accounts a great tool that companies can use to build their own applications, facilitate interactions with customers, and even establish their own e-shop platform on WeChat.

Corporate Accounts

Corporate accounts—also known as *Enterprise Accounts*—instead of mass broadcasting to a large audience, are generally used as an internal communication tool within a company. Such accounts simplify the company's management and communication system. They are mobile office automation systems and are used to record employee attendance, track team projects, form department groups, and send messages to staff. They can even encrypt messages in order to prevent confidential data leakage. Corporate accounts are closed communities, because they can only be accessed with an invitation. For external marketing purposes, it is best to open a subscription account or a service account.

A few tips:

It is best to set up a service account unless you are a media company. As an international brand, you can register an official WeChat account in three cases:

- You have a registered business in China.
- You register with a local third-party agent who will be the owner of your account.
- You submit an application to WeChat directly and guarantee a minimum expenditure of RMB 200,000.

Key Functions of Official Accounts

Official accounts provide all sorts of functions to help businesses and brands to conduct their marketing campaigns.

Content Broadcasting

The most prominent feature is content broadcasting. Messages and articles are the main way brands share information and communicate with their followers on WeChat. There are five types of content available:

- Articles
- Text
- Images
- Audio
- Video

Articles are the most common and most sophisticated type of broadcast content. They can be made up of text, images, videos, and audios. An article can be viewed as a webpage. At the bottom of each article, users can click to like it or check out the number of views and comments from other users. Such articles can also be shared on a contact's Moments page, as well as on external platforms like Qzone or Microsoft OneNote. This means that, even if users have not subscribed to your company's account, they can still read your articles and share them. As explained earlier, subscription accounts allow account holders to publish once every 24 hours, while the posting frequency of service accounts is much lower—four times per month—independently of the content format. Although you can combine multiple articles and publish up to eight articles each time, they will be presented as a single post on the user interface. Please note that it is not a hard-and-fast rule that you should publish articles every day or that you should post several articles each time. As long as your articles are high quality, you can choose the frequency that suits best your brand strategy and marketing needs. In 2018, WeChat has announced that it will be soon providing a dedicated application for official accounts that will have extended functions and bring additional advantages to vendors.

Comments Under Articles

In addition to liking and sharing articles, users can leave comments under these articles. After users post a comment, it is not displayed immediately. Comments are collected for review by the management backend and can only be displayed when the account holder moves it to the *featured comments* section. Account holders can reply to users' comments. Replies are displayed under the original comment and can be seen by everyone. To make users feel appreciated, it is important that you keep a highly conversational tone and use engaging comments in your replies. This encourages users to post more comments and is a great way for official accounts to monitor and control publicly displayed comments.

Automatic Messages

To improve communication and encourage user engagement, official account holders can create automatic messages. Such messages can be sent in the form of text, images, videos, or voice messages. This category includes welcome messages, autoreply messages, and keyword-based autoreplies. Welcome messages are automatically sent from an official account after a user subscribes to it. It can be a long or short text, voice message, or picture. Such messages welcome new subscribers and provide a brief introduction to the account and its basic functions. Autoreply messages are the second category of automatic messages and appear when a user sends an enquiry to the official account. Generally, account holders leverage this function to let users know that their message is well received and will be answered as soon as possible. Finally, the third category of autoreply messages is more sophisticated. Keyword autoreplies are designated replies that appear only after users send a message that contains certain keywords. The rules can be preset by the account holder. This type of messages is very useful for FAQs, as specific rules can be set up, according to the type of question submitted by a user.

One-on-One Communication

Users who follow official accounts may send direct messages to seek help, make enquires, or complaints. One-on-one communication is a channel that companies and brands can use to build a direct rapport with their followers. Chinese users prefer to chat with merchants directly via official accounts, rather than sending e-mails or making phone calls. From an account holder's perspective, WeChat is essentially a CRM system, allowing them to collect direct feedback from users and deal with their enquiries. To contact a company, users can send private messages to the official account. In addition to autoreplies, merchants also send messages manually for a *live chat*. It is important to know that messages sent to your official account cannot be replied after 48 hours, which means that new messages must be answered very quickly. On top of this, messages are only retained in the system for no more than five days. Chinese consumers are very demanding. They expect an almost instant reply to their enquiries. Therefore, handling users' messages in a professional and timely manner plays a key role there.

Custom Menus

A custom menu can be set up at the bottom of an official account page. Each account is allowed to add three main menus and five submenus under each main menu. When users click on different menus, they usually receive various messages or WeChat articles or are directed to external webpages. Custom menus are particularly useful for service accounts, as more complicated CRM systems can be integrated and different menus can be used for advanced functions like bookings, WeChat stores, and loyalty programs.

User and Content Analysis

Thanks to the account management center, account holders can track their content performance, the article reach, and page views, as well as detailed data such as the number of shares and hyperlink clicks.

Tips

1. Publish up to three articles at a time is the optimal frequency for the average official account holder. Prepare engaging articles and list them in order of importance.
2. A custom menu should include some basic information: brand and product introduction, contact details, sales channels, and customer service channels.
3. Link backend user data to the brand's CRM system or sales conversion tools for better user data tracking and profiling purposes.

Content Strategy

An official account allows businesses to reach their target audience and grow the number of followers by publishing relevant content regularly. The success of any official account is determined by its content and its ability to win the heart of its customers. A well-designed account with valuable content can help a brand stand out and connect with their audience. WeChat articles are generally lengthier and more informative than posts users find on other social media platforms. WeChat users are more likely to share useful content. Emotionally appealing content, offers and discount updates are also very effective. The most popular types of content on WeChat generally fit into the following five categories:

Trending Topics

Hot topics are the most important content type to incorporate into your articles. They can be about a recent movie, a best-selling book, social issues, special occasions, and so on. Plenty of issues are being discussed on social media, so make sure you focus on those that are recent, relevant, and local. Relating an article to hot topics helps grab attention, encourages readership, and stimulates liking and sharing. Most organic followers can find your account after seeing content that has been shared on their friends' Moments page, so it is extremely important to create unique, shareable articles that add character to your brand profile.

Useful Information

Your subscribers want to know that you are an expert in your field, and that your social media account is a good place to get detailed insights on your industry trends and products. Users like articles that teach them something helpful and are more than willing to share them with their friends and relatives. So, this type of posts usually enjoy a high level of engagement and can bring in a lot of new traffic. For example, tutorials with practical tips or extensive lists are popular on WeChat. Brands often give useful tips on how to use their products. This kind of content also helps brands to show that they are professional and strengthens their credibility.

Interactive Content

Many official accounts interact with their followers by sharing opinions, telling jokes, inviting them to participate in discussions, collecting their opinions on a specific topic, or creating a poll to let them vote. This type of interactive content helps trigger discussion and increases the account's traffic. However, such content should be created only after the account has secured a few thousand followers. Otherwise, there will not be much interaction.

Sales

Sales promotions are often posted in the form of articles. However, this information should be embedded in articles about more general topics because users can be easily turned-off by a hard sales approach. If the whole article looks more like a dry newsletter or if it focuses solely on product promotion, it will not hit the right notes with your audience. Sales information should always appear together with other types of content. Most articles contain several types of content. They may start with a trending topic, then have some educational information or fun elements followed by sales information at the end. For instance, the article can start with practical tips on how to use the product, end with sales information, and contain other useful content in the middle. QR codes or purchase links can also be added to facilitate sales.

Brand-Related Content

Brand-related content should contain authentic brand stories and news. It is a good idea to produce some articles about both the history of the brand and the company's latest achievements. This allows Chinese users to get familiar and deepen their understanding of the brand, which, again, leads to enhanced brand loyalty. Companies can also discuss recent product developments to keep their audience intrigued and create anticipation.

Promotion

Launching campaigns on WeChat is the most effective way to increase user engagement. Although WeChat itself does not have a specific function to organize campaigns, companies can still launch their campaigns through articles offering incentives like discounts or giveaways. There are four common campaign types on WeChat that are often combined:

Lucky Draw

Lucky draws are the most popular WeChat campaign on WeChat. Generally, at the end of a WeChat article, a topic is raised for discussion, and readers are encouraged to leave comments or send private messages to the brand's official account. The account holder can then choose the lucky draw winner(s) from the participant list. Lucky draws are popular among Chinese users and very effective in encouraging user interactions, attracting new followers, and increasing their loyalty.

User-Generated Content Collection

Brands often encourage users to create themed photos of themselves with the brand's products and submit them through private message to the brand's account or upload them to a campaign page to win a gift. Also, brands often launch polls for users to vote for their favorite product or pick their favorite products to be displayed in a future advertising campaign. Companies can also cooperate with KOLs (key opinion leaders)—also known as influencers—when launching such campaigns. User-generated content (UGC) is another type of lucky draw. The main difference is that visual UGC is more persuasive than written testimonials or customer reviews. It also helps companies collect original, high-quality content from their followers, which can be used in future marketing campaigns and increases user engagement. It is also good for attracting new subscribers.

H5 Pages and Games

Mobile-friendly webpages made with HTML 5.0—known as H5 pages—have become one of the most popular tools to conduct WeChat campaigns. It is a very popular trend for companies to build H5 pages for event invitations, interactive digital product brochures, branding, and other marketing activities. An H5 page may feature video, audio, complex animation, or 3D effects. Many companies have integrated H5 pages allowing brands to maximize interactivity with their users. A very common practice is to create a mini game for users to play with top players and win gifts. Alternatively, some companies create H5 pages allowing users to create sharable, individualized content. For instance, they can upload photos to their H5 page to view them with special effects or in different formats. H5 pages have proven to be particularly effective when it comes to improving audience engagement and interaction. They have the potential to go viral and can help brands achieve much wider exposure on WeChat.

Sales Campaigns

There are several ways to launch a more sales-driven campaign. Companies can include themed coupons in WeChat articles, which can then be used either online or offline. Before the coupon expires, users usually receive a message reminding them to use it. This establishes two touch points with customers: the moment the coupon is collected and the moment before it expires.

Flash sales campaigns (discounted sales of designated items for a limited time) are another popular tactic among marketers. They sell limited editions as a special prize to boost sales or offer benefits for purchases over a defined amount. This kind of campaigns help drive traffic from official accounts to online stores. People love special offers and discounts, so sales campaigns are another great way to attract new followers and increase brand loyalty.

Tips for Launching a WeChat Campaign

1. Give each campaign a clear focus and objective. Before initiating a campaign, first determine its goal. The goal can be to boost sales, increase brand awareness, or collect user information to build a database.
2. Offering incentives is a key way to achieve higher engagement. The more complex the campaign rules, the better the gifts users expect to be. Offer gifts that are symbolic and related to your brand, industry, or your campaign theme.
3. Plan a suitable duration for the campaign. A WeChat campaign usually lasts for up to one week in order to achieve optimal exposure and generate participation.
4. Launching campaigns for special events or festivals increases exposure and attracts a larger audience. Weekends, holidays, and national festivals are the best time to launch campaigns. To make sure that you do not miss any important dates for promotion, create a marketing calendar highlighting major holidays like the Chinese New Year, the Mid-Autumn Festival, the Dragon Boat Festival, the 11.11 Festival, and so on.
5. When it comes to H5 campaigns, always test them before the official launch and monitor the various stages of the campaign for possible technical issues or bugs that might allow cheating, especially for campaigns offering special prizes and incentives.

6. Regulations for WeChat campaigns are quite strict. For example, companies cannot launch any campaigns that ask people to follow certain WeChat accounts in return for incentives.

Cooperation with KOLs and Influencers

Engaging influencers and KOLs is one of the fastest and most effective ways to promote an official account on WeChat, post content, or launch WeChat campaigns. KOLs have their own crowd of followers and subscribers who view their opinions and suggestions as credible and influential. Many influencers excel in driving online sales, sharing brand information, offering code discounts, or launching the whole campaign by themselves. Collaborating with bloggers can help raise brand awareness, increase the brand's follower base, and contribute to the brand's credibility. Unlike bloggers in other parts of the world, Chinese bloggers do not engage in direct sales. With the expansion of official WeChat accounts, their followers continue to grow, increasing the influence, value, and income of KOLs. Compared with other advertising options, KOL promotion is often, but not always, less costly. The price of WeChat KOL cooperation differs primarily based on their industry, content quality, interest category, follower base, and popularity. The larger the fan base, the higher the content quality and the higher the cost of a contract.

Types of KOLs on WeChat

Most KOLs have subscription accounts, and these can be found by searching within WeChat. There are naturally different categories of KOLs and influencers. They have official accounts that can be divided into two broad categories: individual accounts and agency-managed accounts. Micro-KOLs on WeChat typically have less than 10,000 views per post. Mid-size KOLs average around 50,000 views, while top KOLs have more than 100,000 views per post.

Individual Accounts

As the names suggests, individual accounts are created and managed by individuals. WeChat does not verify accounts opened by individuals.

Individual accounts help brands to maintain a good rapport with their followers. Individual account holders are considered reliable authorities when they make product recommendations. These bloggers have stricter standards when choosing brands to cooperate with because they need to maintain their content quality and reputation. When brands cooperate with established individual account bloggers, they can attract a sizeable audience and increase customer loyalty.

Agency-Managed Accounts

As the name suggests, agency-managed accounts are managed by a company or an agency that is listed on their profile page. This type of accounts are verified, and oftentimes, there are several verified accounts under the same name. WeChat allows a maximum of 50 official accounts to be verified under one brand name. These accounts are open to advertising and are more likely to engage with hard sales and marketing approaches. If an agency has several official accounts, companies can consider advertising on more than one account. Agencies usually offer discounts if companies choose to advertise through more than one of their accounts.

KOL Prices and Payment

WeChat KOLs are generally more expensive to hire than Weibo KOLs. Micro-KOLs normally charge between 3,000 RMB and 15,000 RMB per post per article. Mid-tier KOLs' prices range from 15,000 RMB to 80,000 RMB. Asking KOLs to create themselves text or visual content or place the brand's post in a prominent position naturally requires higher prices. The majority of KOLs and their agencies accept payments through Alipay. Bank transfers are also accepted, though not preferred, as they often take a longer time to clear. Most bloggers in China require 100 percent prepayment and will only begin promoting your posts after full payment has been received. For smaller businesses, with a contracted amount that is below 15,000 RMB, KOLs rarely sign official agreements. The usual procedure is to negotiate the terms and pay the full amount prior to the work commencing. Please note that most individual bloggers do not issue legal receipts—called *fapiao* in Mandarin—unless you request one. A legal receipt costs about 10 percent on top of the contract amount.

Finding WeChat KOLs

While WeChat does not have a section where all bloggers are listed, there are three main ways to search for KOLs on WeChat:

WeChat's Native Search

You can type keywords in the search bar and choose to display only results for official accounts. Then, you will see a list of official accounts based on the keyword search.

KOL Search Engines

There are various KOL search engines such as Sougou, Search Engine for WeChat, NeeRank, Robin8, gsdata.cn. Users can search for KOLs by using keywords and categories. Filters are provided to help further narrow the search. These databases allow users to get the latest data on the total article views, the number of followers, as well as other important statistics. Sometimes, the price range of these KOLs is displayed there too. An alternative platform is PARKLU, which is a KOL matchmaking platform where companies can post information on the campaigns they wish to launch, available budget, and timeline, then select from the list of the KOLs who have applied for collaboration.

KOL Agencies

There are three main KOL agencies in China.

- Louis Communication
- Gushan Culture
- Yaxian Advertising

In addition to these agencies, there is a plethora of companies managing KOL databases. Users can select KOLs by interest category, industry, and promotion budget. They can also check their number of followers and subscribers and get service quotes. After you have identified matching KOLs, it is important that you check their online reputation, previous posts, and articles to see the number of views, likes, and comments.

You can also ask KOLs to provide screenshots of their account performance statistics from their account management page to get a better idea of their audience and potential reach, in case you choose to work with them. When working with KOLs, it is easy to decide which promotional method works best to maximize exposure. There are five common methods companies use when working with KOLs on WeChat: product placement, product reviews, sponsored campaigns, WeChat advertising, and Moments ads.

Product Placement and Advertorials

Native advertising—also known under the term *advertorial*—is the most common way for brands to work with WeChat KOLs. In this case, KOLs prepare an article about a topic in their usual style that features the product or use images featuring the product in the article. Because the articles are original and engaging, readers are less likely to click away. For a sales campaign, brands usually ask KOLs to insert a sales link at the end of the article. Companies integrate different tracking codes in the purchase links distributed to various KOLs to measure their effectiveness and calculate the final commission based on a PPC (pay per click) pricing model.

Product Reviews

For companies, product reviews are the most effective way to introduce their services and products. As many KOLs are experts in their field, they can produce reliable and informative product reviews and compare similar products. Their product reviews are often paired with tutorials and giveaway campaigns or links to the product's online sales page. Companies that partner with WeChat KOLs who like their products can reach a larger audience and see a noticeable increase in sales.

Sponsored Campaigns and Co-Branding

Brands sponsoring influencers to launch campaigns is another popular practice. KOLs introduce the campaign and offer gifts sponsored by the brand. They can drive traffic to the brand's official account by integrating the brand's official account QR code at the bottom of the article. It is important to work together with Chinese KOLs. They retain their style, voice, and approach while engaging in promotional activities.

Sometimes, brands co-create a product with a famous blogger or a KOL and sell it as a limited edition. An example of this is the co-branding between Givenchy and Mr. Bags (a famous WeChat KOL) in early 2017. About 80 limited edition bags worth 1.2 million RMB sold out in 12 minutes. After this successful campaign, Mr. Bags followed up with similar cross-over promotions, working with other luxury brands such as Chloé and Burberry. A growing number of fashion KOLs have their own WeChat stores or mini programs for e-commerce purposes. Companies can offer special editions of their products in the KOL's WeChat e-shop. It is a good strategy to work with various KOLs for your first campaign in China in order to establish a baseline for results. Choose the best-performing KOLs for your next campaign. Repeat this process until you are left with three to five bloggers who you are happy to work with regularly. It is best to have a long-term cooperation with quality KOLs. If you work with them on a regular basis, their followers will get used to your brand and will be more responsive to promotions.

WeChat Advertising

Thanks to the personalization of digital advertising in China, consumers are twice as likely to click on an ad, compared to the global average. This huge number of active users has made WeChat a battlefield where marketers and advertisers promote their products. However, advertising is not open to all official accounts, neither to all industries. Only companies with verified official accounts in specific industries can apply for advertising campaigns on WeChat.

Currently, WeChat offers two major advertising options: Moments ads and account ads. A new advertising option for mini programs is currently being tested.

Moments Ads

As explained earlier, WeChat's Moments page is similar to Facebook's wall and news feed. Users use this space to share their status updates, articles, photos, and so on. WeChat ads look like normal Moments posts with an additional *sponsored* tag in the upper-right corner. Moments ads can be used to promote an official account, publicize a campaign, or encourage users to download an application, distribute coupons, or launch location-based promotions. For Moments ads, marketers can define their target audience by industry, location, gender, educational level, marital status, and so on.

Display Formats

Starting from 2017, Moments ads have two new formats. One is a card format with a larger space where visual elements are displayed. This enlarges the ad, making it more appealing and eye-catching and also enables it to convey more information on the featured product. Clicking on the card directs viewers to an H5 page or a native advertising page. The second format is an advanced ad format with two buttons, which enables advertisers to showcase two sets of advertising materials in one single ad. Users can click on either button to view different advertisements. Moments ads allow mutual interactions between brands and followers because the latter can like and comment under the ad.

Pricing

Moments ads use the CPM (pay per mille) pricing model. Advertisers are charged per 1,000 views. There are two main purchasing schemes: scheduling and auction.

Scheduling	Auction
Ensures a certain amount of exposure is based on the allocated budget.	This scheme is suitable for advertisers who need flexibility in terms of advertising time and constant ad customization.
CPM pricing model.	
Price is location-based: first-tier cities, second-tier cities, and third-tier and smaller cities. RMB 50–150/M for text and image ads. RMB 60–180/M for video and audio ads.	Price is location-based: first-tier cities, second-tier cities, and third-tier and smaller cities. RMB 30–300/M for text, video, and audio ads.
Minimum budget: 50,000 RMB per campaign.	**Minimum budget:** 1,000 RMB per day.

Source: *China Internet Watch, 2018.*

Account Ads

WeChat offers an alternative advertising channel: account ads. Currently, there are three main types of account ads:

- Footer ads
- Video ads
- Exchange ads

Like Moments ads, account ads can be used to promote an official account or a campaign, encourage users to download an application, or distribute coupons. Account ads also allow brands to advertise products from their WeChat store so that users can find out more or directly purchase the item by clicking on the ad.

Display Formats
Pricing
Mini Program Ads

WeChat has recently released a new feature for its mini programs: allowing advertisers to bid for ad space in the *Mini Programs Nearby* section. It is, however, under internal testing, and WeChat has not yet officially announced detailed pricing, neither its specific procedures. When WeChat users open the *Mini Programs Nearby* list, they can see a list of mini programs based on their current location. These mini program ads also appear when people use the search function. For example, when users search for keywords like *Thai restaurant* or *hotel*, related mini programs appear. WeChat's advertising options allow marketers to choose the option that suits best their budget and promotion goals and to showcase their products to target audiences. They also offer an effective way to increase brand exposure and accumulate new subscribers.

How to Start Selling on WeChat

As mentioned before, each WeChat user has a personal WeChat Wallet that is linked to their actual bank account. With their WeChat Wallet, users can engage in the following types of transactions:

Money Transfers

The most common use of the digital wallet is to transfer money to other WeChat users or send red packets. Money can be transferred to a seller's account or to family and friends' accounts. As explained earlier, red packets are a Chinese tradition that consists in offering small amounts of money in red envelopes to friends and family at Chinese New Year. It is the equivalent of gift-giving at Christmas in the West. WeChat was the first to make this tradition virtual in 2014. This helped increase the number of WeChat users by millions. WeChat red packets have evolved and are now sent on various kinds of special occasions, such as family celebrations and birthdays, or as a quick way to transfer small sums to friends. In 2017, Chinese users sent on average 28 red packets or 580 RMB per month. Users also sent 46 billion red packets during the Chinese New Year festival, while more than 6.4 billion were sent during the Mid-Autumn Festival of the same year. Companies can leverage this function, as official accounts with a WeChat Pay account can send red packets to their followers on special occasions.

Daily Tasks

Apart from money transfers and red packets, WeChat Pay provides a wide range of payment services. For instance, users can use WeChat Wallet to repay credit card debts, purchase financial services, and donate to charities. Utility bills—electricity, phone, water, TV, and so on—can also be paid using WeChat Pay; it can also be used for parking and traffic tickets. It can also be used to pay for city services such as settling tax bills or making medical appointments.

Third-Party Operators

In WeChat Wallet, there is a section at the bottom that says *powered by third-party operator*. This section features major tourism, hospitality, transportation, and e-commerce brands. These are Tencent partners, and this section brings them traffic and also offers users a streamlined payment option. For example, JD.com has its own section that allows users to access their online store from within the wallet. Other well-known brands featured there include popular taxi-hailing services, online food delivery platforms, train and flight booking services, and leading online travel agencies, which offer group-buying services and other business services. By partnering up with these brands, WeChat has successfully established a solid service network and cemented its presence in the daily life of Chinese users. Since late 2016, WeChat has moved beyond partnerships, investors, and stockholders. They created a separate section called *Limited Time Promotion* where brands are featured for a short period of time. Starbucks was the first company to benefit. Since 2016, customers can pay through WeChat in more than 2,400 Starbucks stores across China. In 2017, Starbucks and WeChat co-organized an O2O (online to offline) campaign called *Say it with Starbucks*. Customers could buy gift cards by clicking a Starbucks icon displayed in their wallet and could also send them to friends through a message. The cards granted holders a free coffee in any Starbucks store in Mainland China. Recently, Mobike, a stationless bike-sharing system, has also partnered up with WeChat. The Mobike button in the digital wallet is linked to its mini program, thus helping users find bikes nearby. Scanning the QR code on the bike unlocks it automatically. Mobike conducted a 30-day free-ride campaign when the promotion launched so that users could get familiar with this service and share free rides with their WeChat friends.

WeChat Pay for Companies and Merchants

This novel payment method is safe, quick, and simple and has revolutionized shopping and consumer interactions in China. Merchants and brands can use their WeChat Pay account for online and offline transactions. Especially for offline transactions, payments are usually made by scanning QR codes provided by merchants. WeChat Pay offers four major features for brands and merchants:

WeChat Pay Merchant Functions

1. **In-app Web-based Payments**
   This function is available for service accounts, government, and corporate accounts. When brands or merchants broadcast promotions

or product messages to their followers through their official WeChat account, they have their WeChat Pay enabled, and followers can purchase the products on the company's WeChat e-shop instantly. When users purchase directly within WeChat, they can complete the payment without leaving the app. In-app web-based payments are suitable for payments within official accounts, on Moments pages, and on chat pages. Customers can pay with their wallet balance or directly from their linked bank card. After confirming the payment amount using their password or fingerprint recognition, they receive a payment notification. They are then directed back to the merchant's homepage and receive more detailed payment information later.

2. **In-app Payments**

Merchants can use WeChat Pay's software development kit to integrate WeChat Pay into their applications. For example, if users make a purchase on an external e-commerce platform application on their mobile device, they can choose to pay through WeChat once on the payment page. WeChat processes the payment and directs the user to the previous app.

3. **QR Code Payments**

QR codes can be created for different items. After scanning these codes, users can access product information and choose different payment options. QR code payments can also be used for payments on desktop and laptop sites. After being directed to the payment page and choosing to pay via WeChat, a special QR payment code will be generated by the vendor for users to scan. Note that this feature is available for corporate accounts, service accounts, media, as well as government accounts.

To complete transactions quickly, merchants can scan the payment code shown by customers on the Quick Pay page. In offline stores, for instance, users show the payment code in their WeChat Wallet for vendors to scan, in which case, the payment is processed automatically. Quick Pay is equally convenient for offline vendors like convenience stores or supermarkets where payment is processed face to face.

4. **Weixin Checkout**

WeChat helps vendors generate QR codes, which they can print and place to their stores. This allows customers to scan those codes when making purchases. Weixin Checkout is a great tool for vendors who do not possess programming skills. After scanning the QR code, customers confirm the amount with the merchant and input it in the interface. They then confirm that amount and complete the payment. A message with transaction details is later received by the merchant.

The *follow after payment* setting allows merchants to direct their offline traffic to their online account. This is a default setting for Quick Pay. However, this feature is not automatic, and the settings for different payment methods are different. The *follow after payment* feature can only be activated when the amount is above five RMB (0.80 U.S. dollars), and it is only available to established brands when the in-app payment option is being used. Subscription accounts cannot access the *follow after payment* setting. Service accounts with over 500,000 followers can benefit from this feature. WeChat Pay vendors are normally charged a commission that varies, based on the industry and product category.

WeChat E-Commerce: WeChat Stores

A WeChat e-commerce presence is becoming the norm for all companies. However, it is particularly useful for brands that do not have yet a physical presence in China, as WeChat enables cross-border purchases through WeChat payments. People tend to think that it is not possible for foreign companies outside China to set up a WeChat store. It is! WeChat stores do not get organic traffic though. They need to be promoted. After a company establishes their store on WeChat, they can link it to their official account menu. To buy a product, users can click the custom menu linked to the store to view and choose products using WeChat Pay. The whole purchasing process can be done within WeChat, so the conversion rates increase. Vendors can attract customers with discounts and special offers.

Types of Online Stores on WeChat

There are four main types of WeChat stores:

1. **Official WeChat Stores**
   Verified WeChat service accounts can create this type of platform on their account management page for free.

2. **Stores Hosted by a Third Party**

   There are service providers that enable integration within WeChat. Brands build their store on these platforms and link it to their official account. Most subscription account holders use this platform to build their online stores as the official store function is not available to them. You can usually build the online store for free, but WeChat often charges a deposit and/or management fees. Well-known third-party platforms include Youzhan, WalktheChat, Weidian, and Weimob.

3. **Stores on External E-Commerce Platforms**

   This type of stores include mainstream platforms like JD.com. Taobao, and Tmall stores. These cannot be integrated into WeChat, as they belong to Tencent's main rival, Alibaba. A company can link to its own official e-commerce platform, but the major drawback is that this takes more time, effort, and financial resources to develop and maintain.

4. **Mini-Program Online Stores**

   With the rise of mini programs, companies now have another option to build their online stores. The WeChat Shop Mini Program is available on the account management page to all official accounts. Advantages include simple procedures, low development costs, perfect integration with WeChat Pay, and access to the Cards and Offers function. Because mini programs are a built-in function in WeChat, a good traffic flow is ensured. This type of store can be linked to official accounts. Companies can broadcast articles with sales information and launch campaigns encouraging users to visit their stores. Customers can also pay via WeChat Pay, which is always there to smooth out the conversion of user traffic into actual sales.

Cooperating with KOLs and Distributors

Brands can normally launch their online stores to sell their products directly to customers. Alternatively, as sales on WeChat are heavily supported by social media and KOLs, brands can cooperate with distributors and KOLs who have already established their own stores on WeChat. Companies can offer special products for sale or launch flash sales campaigns on their stores.

Cards and Coupons

This feature plays a supporting role in the Chinese e-commerce ecosystem. The *Cards and Coupons* function allows brands with verified official accounts to distribute cards and coupons to their customers. This includes membership cards, vouchers, and prepaid cards. These are distributed by an instant message, as well as through articles, automatic messages, H5 pages, offline QR codes, and via WeChat Shake. Users can store their cards in the *Cards and Offers* section after collecting them on their personal WeChat page on WeChat. They can use them when they shop offline or online and receive a notification before unused coupons expire. Some coupons and cards can be shared with friends and contacts, thus creating viral spread potential.

WeChat Brand Zone

WeChat launched Brand Zone in late 2017. It is a new search function. Some international luxury brands such as Louis Vuitton, Gucci, Cartier, Longchamp, and Michael Kors have already made use of it. Users can access the *Discover* section, click on *Search*, and put a brand name as the search keyword. At the top of the search results is the Brand Zone where users can see two tabs. The top tab is connected to an online store and also showcases the brand's latest collection, while the second tab usually goes to the brand's official account. This feature allows brands to get extra exposure from organic search and drive user traffic from one section to another. Users' ever-growing dependence on WeChat Pay signals a great opportunity and an urgent need for change. Both offline and online retailers need to enable consumers to pay via WeChat and help them adapt to a changing e-commerce landscape based on WeChat as the leading social platform.

CRM with WeChat

Brands need to approach WeChat from a CRM and service innovation perspective; otherwise, their WeChat account will not be anything more than a spam box. Companies want to map their WeChat followers to a CRM system of their own. There is no *one solution fits all* approach when it comes to CRM—especially China CRM!—which is why customizable and integration-friendly CRM solutions are the way to go. Having social media CRM in place will help you understand your customers and followers much better and get familiar with their digital trail, which, again, will help you provide a better and more personalized service and content. Unlike Facebook and Twitter, the method used by WeChat does not allow brands to identify who users are outside of WeChat. The need to link a user's open ID to an e-mail address or mobile phone is generally the starting point for moving CRM off of WeChat. Also, each WeChat user is limited to a 100 unique tags. If you are looking for a scalable way to manipulate tags, this is not the WeChat backend. Once you have done a good job tagging your followers and subscribers, the primary value is for targeted outbound marketing segmentation, which usually requires a third party.

As WeChat enables brands and companies to communicate directly through official accounts, it can be used as an effective CRM tool that companies can use to communicate. WeChat allows companies to collect and analyze customer data, preferences, and consumption trends. There are plenty of third-party CRM tools offering all sorts of advanced functions. Integrated with those systems, such as WeChat Now, WeixinHost, Capillary, and others, WeChat can help brands and merchants manage inquiries from users and provide better, more customized services. A multi-customer solutions tool allows several staff members to talk to different customers at the same time, so that they do not have to wait long to have their questions answered.

Loyalty Programs

Loyalty programs are the most common type of CRM service. Having a loyalty program integrated into a brand's official WeChat account, users can sign up for membership, log in to accumulate credit, collect coupons, purchase discounted items, and enjoy other members-only privileges. These programs are widely used by retailers, hotels, and food and beverage brands. There is, however, a lot more that CRM tools can do for brands. Users can, for example, order food using a brand's online delivery official account. For tourism, customers can check out the available dates and make bookings in advance. Location-based services can also be enabled to further assist their search. For instance, users can share their current location with an official account and receive recommendations for nearby stores and e-map navigation directions. There are lots of options available merchants can use to manage customer relationships in addition to basic monitoring and interactions. Rather than responding to customers in a passive way, make good use of powerful third-party tools to collect the data that you need and use it to better understand your customers. Customers demand timely communication and open conversations with companies, but that is not everything. Improving your products and services should be a key goal, especially when there are great tools that can help you better understand your customers' needs.

Mini Programs Overview

Mini programs are embedded cloud-based applications that operate within the WeChat system. They are apps within the app. WeChat aims to become a full, independent operating system. In addition to messaging, social media feeds, mobile payments, and games, it has developed its own built-in web browser, and now, through the mini programs function it launched in late 2016, its own sub-apps. In fact, mini programs have been one of the biggest disruptors in Chinese social media and China's e-commerce industry since their creation. When Tencent officially launched the mini program platform in late 2016, it was considered a turning point for WeChat and a milestone for mobile operating systems. Industry experts predict that WeChat will soon compete with Android and iOS as another major mobile operating system. Although they are more limited compared with full-function applications, mini programs remain very valuable for brands; they can be used to nurture virtual communities, launch creative campaigns, and promote their physical stores. Also, mini programs are much easier to develop than more complex applications. They can be used to test market viability and gather feedback without the need for heavy investment. Their huge user base and sharing features ensure considerable usage.

The term *app* is avoided to differentiate them from Android and Apple products. Because mini programs are built inside WeChat's massive ecosystem, they offer great convenience to consumers who are able to access and use these programs, without leaving the main WeChat application. Using those mini apps means that users do not have to download other applications, saving phone storage and optimizing their overall user experience. Within months, mini programs have cemented their place in China's online ecosystem, leaving many industry insiders surprised by how fast they are growing. According to a new report released in June 2018, there are currently a total of one million mini programs, that is, nearly double compared with the 580,000 in January 2018. In addition to that, the number of daily active users has reached 280 million and keeps growing. Upon hearing these incredible figures, companies might feel rushed to build a mini program. It is, however, important to understand the fundamental trends and traits and what these can mean specifically for their brand, their products, and whether they truly serve their China market strategy.

Map of the WeChat mini program 小程序 Ecosystem

1. **Sharing is the number one way users enter and discover mini programs**

   WeChat being a closed ecosystem—just as it is often difficult for users to discover official accounts—can be equally challenging to draw users to your mini program. To address this problem, WeChat has been continuously adding new gateways for users to discover

Traditional WeChat vs mini program usage during a day

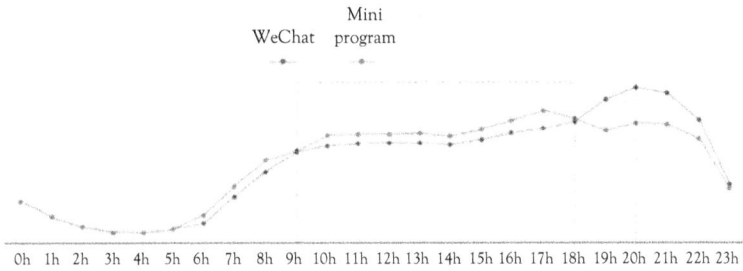

Source: Jisu app's survey of 50,000 mini program.

and access their mini programs. Yet, despite all these options, from January to June 2018, the most common way to enter a mini program was through a mini program card shared in a chat group or on WeChat Moments—with 34.6 percent of users accessing official accounts in this manner.

2. Retention rates are increasing

Once users have discovered your mini program, you need to keep them coming back, and unfortunately, this is not easy to do. The

E-commerce mini-programs industry distribution

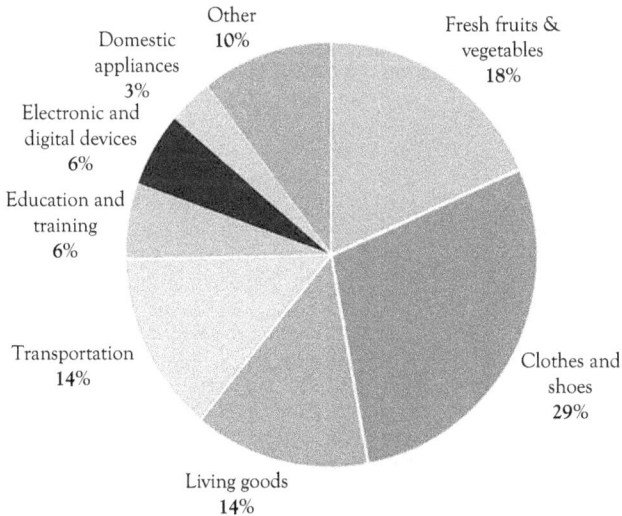

Source: Jisu app's survey of 50,000 mini program.

good news is that, as of June 2018, average user retention rates were significantly higher than in 2017, with next-day retention rates increasing from 13.2 percent to 25.5 percent, and seven-day retention rates increasing from 3.1 percent in 2017 to 13.5 percent in 2018. It is important to keep in mind that, although retention rates keep increasing, they still remain quite low. When it comes to mini program-based e-commerce, companies need to find ways to encourage user engagement. This includes launching loyalty programs and selling limited edition items exclusively on mini programs, as well as adding new merchandise and consistently updating content.

Only 3% of users will come back to mini programs after the first week

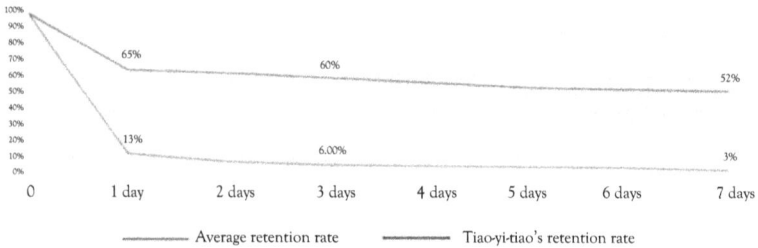

Source: Jisu app's survey of 50,000 mini program.

Time spent using Mini Programs in 2017
(Minutes per day)

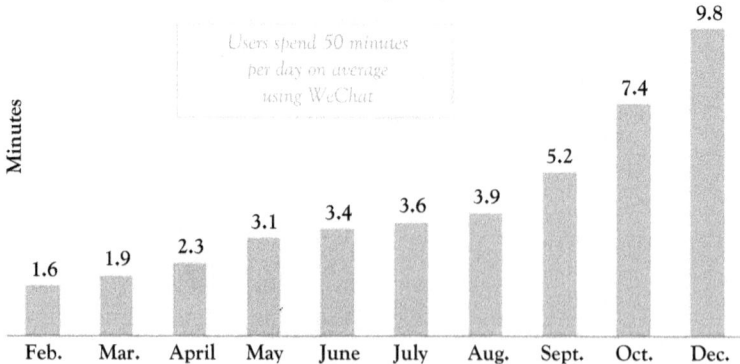

Source: Jisu app's survey of 50,000 mini program.

How many times do users open Mini Programs in a week?

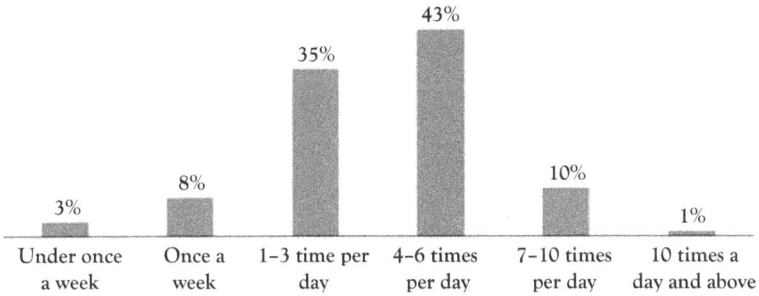

			43%		
	35%				
				10%	
8%					
3%					1%

Under once a week	Once a week	1–3 time per day	4–6 times per day	7–10 times per day	10 times a day and above

Source: Jisu app's survey of 50,000 mini program.

3. Mini program user demographics

According to a recent report, the average age of mini programs users is 29 years old. However, this number might soon increase, considering that the most noticeable change between 2017 and 2018 was the increase in mini program users from the 18–24 years age group, from 17 percent in 2017 to 24 percent in 2018. The largest number of mini program users is currently represented by the 31–35 years age group. When it comes to total usage, the male to female ratio is almost even, 49 percent and 51 percent, respectively. For specific types of mini programs though, the gender ratio is significantly skewed. Most importantly, e-commerce mini program users are predominantly female, accounting for 67 percent of users. When gender ratios are further broken down into specific types of merchants and product categories, the most dramatic imbalance occurs for vertical retailers, that is, brands selling their own products and whose mini program customers are 95 percent female and only 5 percent male. When it comes to users' educational level, 68 percent hold a bachelor's or a higher degree.

The top five cities with the greatest number of mini program users are: Beijing, Guangzhou, Shanghai, Shenzhen, and Chengdu. Independently of industry, company type, and product category, the percentage of mini program users coming from first-tier coastal cities remain the highest. Therefore, at an average of age of 29 years, with a relatively high educational level and living in first-tier cities, mini program users are an excellent target group for foreign brands selling high-end goods. Also, companies targeting female users will very likely witness a bigger success.

50% of Mini program users come from 1st and 2nd Tier Cities

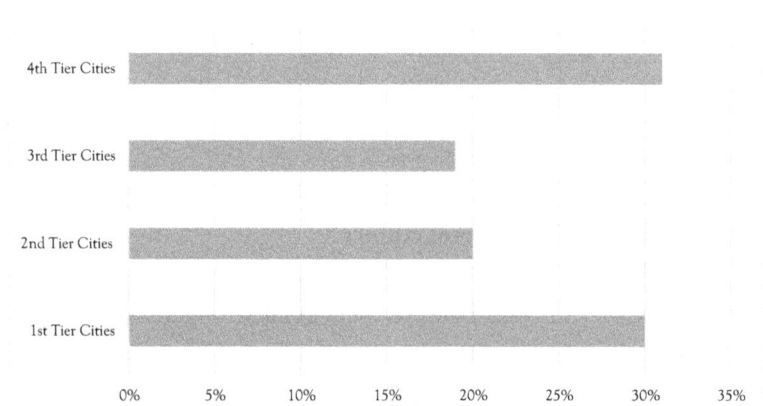

Source: Jisu App Survey of 50,000 mini program users, Walk the Chat.

Top 10 cities using mini programs

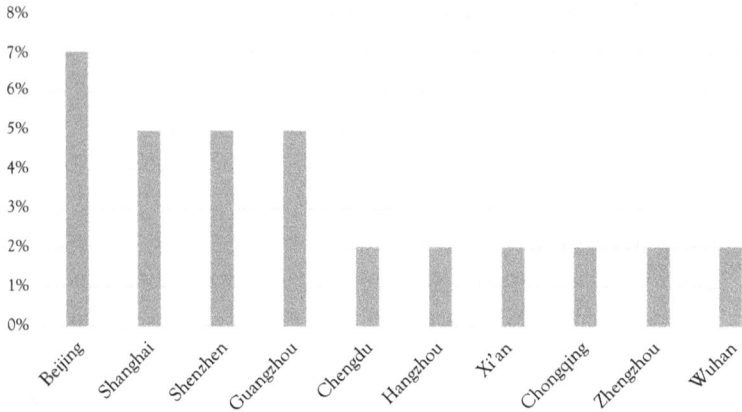

Source: Statista, 2018.

Age distribution of mini program users in 2017

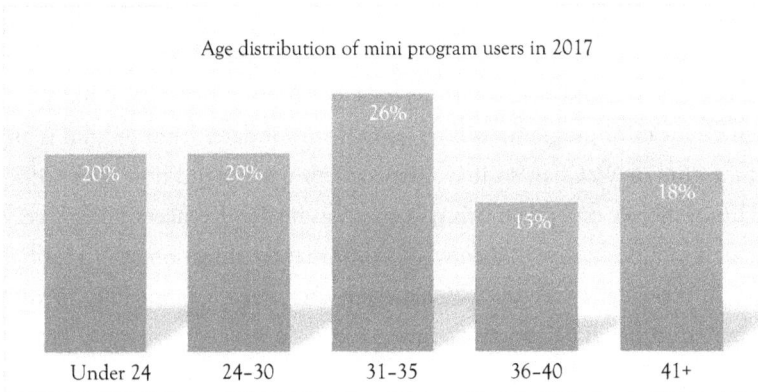

Source: Jisu App Survey of 50,000 mini program users, Walk the Chat.

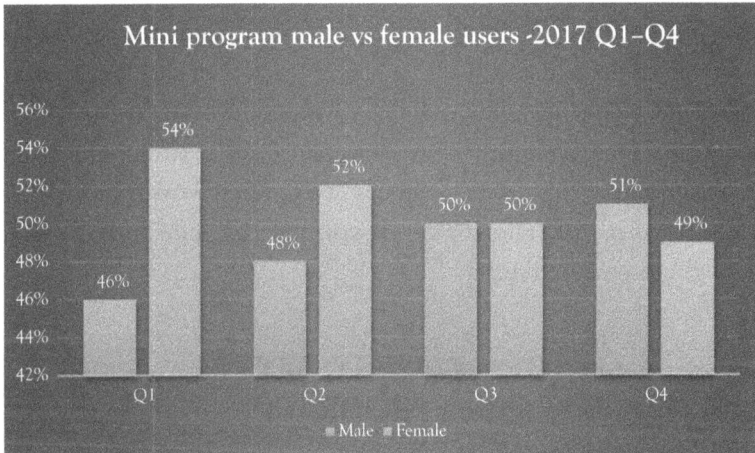

Source: Jisu App Survey of 50,000 mini program users, Walk the Chat.

Mini Programs for Business

From an instant messaging app, WeChat has evolved into China's most widely used platform. But, that is not all. Tencent has expressed its commitment to making WeChat the only platform users will need on their smartphones. WeChat is working to achieve this goal with their mini programs, that is, by creating apps within the app. Mini programs were introduced in 2017 and more than 580,0000 mini programs have been developed since, with 170 million monthly active users. These programs cover 20 industries and more than 200 sub-categories. International brands like KFC, Tesla, and Coach have already launched their own mini programs. The format is changing incredibly fast. These numbers are growing very rapidly, so anything that is currently being said and written about mini programs will be quickly out of date. Mini programs are the future of WeChat, so it is important to understand how they work. China's mobile ecosystem being in constant flux and Tencent being a very dynamic and adaptive company, it is clear that the direction of this format is still evolving. Even the WeChat team themselves cannot fully predict where things will be in a year's time.

How to Use Mini Programs for E-Commerce

E-commerce is by far the hottest mini program category. The WeChat team has worked to produce a framework so that brands can easily build e-commerce stores that actually duplicate the sort of shopping experience that Chinese users are comfortable with from years of using Taobao and Tmall. Many companies have streamlined the checkout process in detail and supercharged mini programs in a variety of ways, which, when added together, make sales conversion easier through mini programs than through standard web stores.

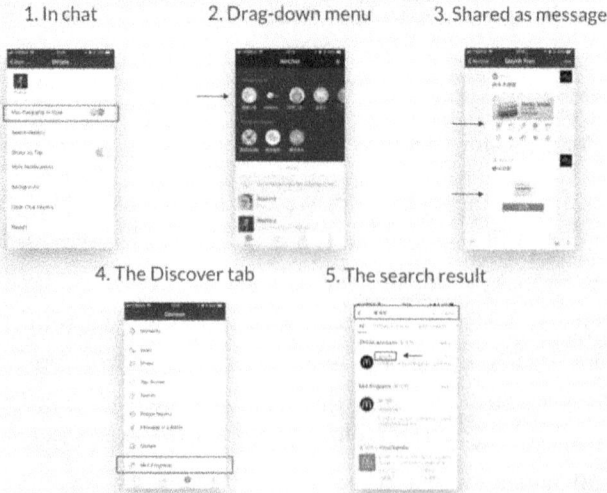

TOP 5 WAYS TO ACCESS MINI PROGRAMS

1. In chat   2. Drag-down menu   3. Shared as message

4. The Discover tab   5. The search result

Gaining Access and Using Mini Programs

There is no mini program page or button. There are several ways to find mini programs to use for the first time. Users can find these programs by searching using keywords, through mini program cards, by scanning special mini program QR codes, or by clicking on links embedded in WeChat articles. Users first have to start using a mini program to activate them on the *Discovery* page. Mini program codes are quite special. They use an exclusive, independent QR code format that can only be created on WeChat, ensuring control and keeping them within the WeChat ecosystem. The codes can be posted to WeChat Moments or sent to friends. They can be opened by long pressing the code or by scanning it. To access mini programs, you can also use WeChat's search bar or get a QR code or mini program card from a friend or group via chat. Official accounts often link to mini programs, and subscribers receive a notification and can access it by clicking on the message or by clicking on it on the official account's profile page. Users can also access them by clicking on mini program cards that usually can be found in WeChat articles.

Mini programs have accumulated a growing user base and tremendous popularity in less than a year. They can replace a large selection of lightly

How do users access mini programs?

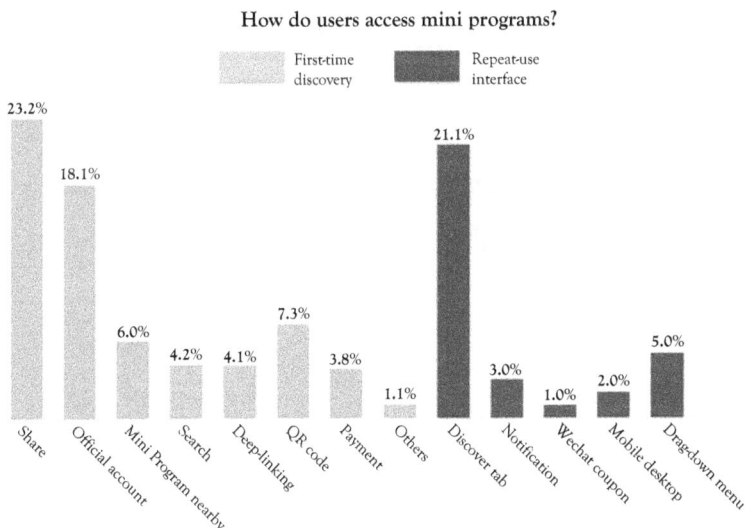

Source: Jisu app's survey of 50,000 mini programs.

used apps or can be used as light versions of current apps. Mini programs can also be used as trial versions of full apps and lead to purchases and more downloads. When it comes to mini program access, the top three ways users entered them were through sharing (33.5 percent), official accounts (31 percent), and through the quick access pull-down at the top of the WeChat app homepage (20 percent).

Remember that official accounts are one of the most popular entry points because a large number of e-commerce mini programs are operated by big brands, WeChat KOLs, and WeMedia (WeChat-operated media). Official accounts enjoy a large existing follower base, which they can use to drive traffic to their mini program stores.

It is important to keep in mind that, unlike with social networks and game-based mini programs, users are not naturally inclined to share e-commerce mini programs. However, sharing being the most popular way, users discover and join mini programs, incorporating incentives for sharing them is key for all brands. In addition to sharing, having a large follower base plays a huge role in a company's ability to drive traffic to their mini programs. Brands with smaller numbers of followers need to focus heavily on user retention and *shareability*.

Likehood of sharing mini programs by mini program type

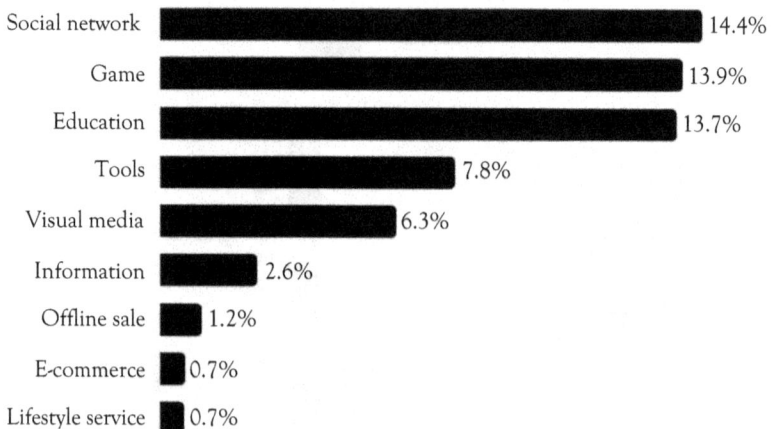

Social network	14.4%
Game	13.9%
Education	13.7%
Tools	7.8%
Visual media	6.3%
Information	2.6%
Offline sale	1.2%
E-commerce	0.7%
Lifestyle service	0.7%

Source: IT Consultis

Daily Necessity Tools

Mini programs are the most popular type and cover most daily needs such as translation, geo-location, transportation, polls, and time management. For example, users can use different mini programs to book tickets and check bus and train schedules.

Information and Entertainment

For entertainment-related services, users can check movie reviews and buy theater tickets directly through the mini programs. There is a large number of mini programs for games. Mini programs also allow users to access useful information such as stock market and exchange rates information.

E-Commerce

Brands are now offered the possibility to develop their own e-commerce platform by using mini programs. This option combines low development costs with convenient integration using WeChat Pay and the *Cards and Offers* feature. Given that mini programs are a built-in function in WeChat, stable user traffic is ensured. Mini programs can also be used to launch giveaways, special offers, as well as user-generated content (UGC) collection campaigns to increase brand awareness, interactivity, and help boost sales. As WeChat gradually allows developers to add more multimedia content in their mini programs, and also considering the popularity of live streaming in China, some merchants have even started doing live streaming on mini programs to boost sales. For example, fashion brands launch flash sales campaigns and live streams to showcase the clothes they sell. If viewers are interested, they can select the items, place an instant order, and complete the payment within the mini program.

WeChat-Related Services

Mini programs offer convenience for those who work closely with official accounts. For example, the *Official Account Assistant* mini program shows the latest account statistics and followers' reviews and comments.

This feature offers the account holder the possibility to constantly log in to the desktop version. The Weixin Checkout mini program allows merchants to easily access transaction details. Another useful mini program is *WeChat Index*. It measures the popularity of designated keywords based on their search volume, their appearance in general articles, and their appearance in shared articles on users' Moments pages. Account holders can input keywords and track their popularity over the last 7, 30, or 90 days. This index is a valuable indicator for companies and social media managers because of the platform's huge base of prime demographic users. It can help companies identify emerging trends and decide whether to incorporate them into their social media content, while it also reveals the popularity of a brand or a specific product.

Mini Programs as an O2O Facilitator

Many new features have been added in order to encourage more people to use mini programs. There are two special programs designed to help companies and merchants promote their physical stores and function as O2O (online to offline) facilitators: Store Mini Programs and Mini Programs Nearby.

Store Mini Programs

In early 2017, WeChat launched a new feature called the *Store Mini Program*, which works pretty much like a virtual business card, showing users the basic information about an offline store. Despite its name, it is not currently a mini program, but a feature related to mini programs. Mini programs offered by stores are an effective online-to-offline channel for brands, especially when they want to boost sales in their brick-and-mortar stores. This feature allows brands and merchants holding official accounts to set up store mini programs in a fast and convenient way by simply using their account management page without need for further programming. Basic store information, including the store name, address, contact details, and store photos, is displayed there. It is best to upload photos of the latest products and campaign posters to give customers a quick clear product reference. Membership cards, coupons, and vouchers can also be distributed through store mini programs. Same chain branches are considered different stores and can distribute different cards and coupons from other branches. Account managers can add an interface that allows customers to collect vouchers and membership cards via store mini programs.

Mini Programs Nearby

Imagine this scene: a customer is in a large shopping mall in the center of Shanghai. She stops and takes out her smartphone to check where she can buy a dress for a special occasion. Instead of launching a map, she opens WeChat and goes directly to the *Mini Programs Nearby* section. Before she decides which store to visit, she can look through all the *mini programs nearby* list and check out their products, offers of the day, and campaign information.

In early 2017, WeChat launched the *Mini Programs Nearby* feature that allows brands with offline locations to display their mini programs. When users are near the brand's location, mini programs of nearby businesses automatically show up. This feature enables sellers to reach more potential customers in real time and plays a crucial role in connecting online customers with their offline stores.

The Future of Mini Programs

Mini program features provide new opportunities for brands and merchants and can lead to a win–win situation for both vendors and customers. For companies and merchants, mini programs provide an alternative O2O conversion channel, by connecting online users with offline stores. Unlike offline stores, where many customers leave immediately without leaving any trace, mini programs offer valuable user statistics that can be used by brands for future reference. Mini programs are also a very convenient platform for customers. Based on what we can see today, the future of WeChat will revolve around further developing and improving mini programs. It is no exaggeration to say that mini programs are the future of WeChat. The main question is how far mini programs will go on to impact the rest of China's mobile ecosystem.

Many industry reports on the growth of mini programs in the second half of 2018 predict that:

- There will be three million mini programs.
- The number of daily active users will reach 400 million.
- Retention rates will continue to increase.
- Tencent will continue making it easier for WeChat users to discover and access mini programs.
- Mini program stores will become the new standard for e-commerce in China.

There is a common misconception that every brand that has entered China must have its own official account on WeChat. This is not entirely so. For instance, WeChat is not really for B2B companies. The target audience of such brands is really niche, and the type of information they need to communicate is less interesting for general users. Another false assumption is that brands can rely solely on WeChat, and that their WeChat presence alone can bring them everything they want. WeChat, being a semi-closed platform, maintains a rather intimate relationship between brands and users, which means that, at the initial stage, it might not be the ideal platform to grow followers and gain popularity.

In the beginning of this book, three categories of brands were discussed, based on their China market entry strategy. These were international brands already in China, brands engaging in cross-border e-commerce, and overseas brands serving Chinese customers abroad. Now, we will see how these three company types can use WeChat and discuss the most relevant features and tools for each company type.

International Brands Already Operating in China

This company type is already legally established in China. They possess brick-and-mortar and/or online stores in Mainland China. They employ local staff and are familiar with Chinese consumers and well-adapted to the local e-commerce ecosystem. Many such brands are already known to a large number of Chinese consumers.

1. **Official Account and WeChat Articles**

   For this type of brands, it makes practical sense to have their own official WeChat account. As already explained, however, brands need to think first who their target audience is and whether they can leverage WeChat's features for maximum benefit. Posting on a regular basis is essential to keep the audience engaged. Articles are the most important content type on WeChat so far. Most subscription accounts post up to three articles a day, while service accounts normally post four to five articles per week. These articles are very important for interactive campaigns because brands can encourage users to leave a comment under an article if they want to participate in lucky draws. They usually ask them to share these articles with their contacts or post them on their Moments page in exchange of a prize or a discount.

2. **Custom Menu Bar for CRM**

   WeChat is a great tool for CRM. A big number of third-party CRM tools can be integrated within WeChat as well. Brands can make full use of these features to create a powerful communication channel through one-on-one messaging, loyalty programs, and other services. The platform helps companies collect very valuable user data and helps them build a database for analysis, so that they can better understand customer needs. These CRM-related functions can be incorporated in the custom menu bar, thus allowing users to find the service they are looking for easily when they enter the official account interface.

3. **WeChat Stores and the *Coupons and Cards* Feature**

   WeChat is very well-suited when it comes to driving sales conversions. Brands can embed links to external e-commerce platforms, with the exception of Taobao and Tmall, which belong to the rival, Alibaba. These links can be added at the end of articles, thus allowing interested readers to buy their preferred products. As an alternative, brands can open their own WeChat stores, which can be done using a mini program. Customers can easily access the store and use membership cards and coupons that they have collected virtually. Full compatibility of WeChat stores with the application itself makes the whole process fast and seamless.

Tencent and Alibaba: key areas of competition

AREA	TENCENT	ALIBABA
PAYMENTS	WECHAT PAY (PAY.WEIXIN.QQ.COM)	ALIPAY (ALIPAY.COM)
ECOMMERCE	JD, VIPSHOP (JD.COM, VIP.COM)	TAOBAO, TMALL (TAOBAO.COM TMALL.COM)
SOCIAL	WECHAT, QQ (WEIXIN.QQ.COM, IM.QQ.COM)	WEIBO (WEIBO.COM)
BROWSERS	QQ BROWSER (BROWSER.QQ.COM)	UC BROWSER (UCWEB.COM)
VIDEO	TENCENT VIDEO (V.QQ.COM)	YOUKU, TUDOU (YOUKU.COM, TUDOU.COM)
RETAIL	YONGHUI, CARREFOUR (YONGHUI.COM.CN, CARREFOUR.CN)	SUNING, HEMA (SUNING.COM, FRESHHEMA.COM)
CLOUD	TENCENT CLOUD (CLOUD.TENCENT.COM)	ALI CLOUD (ALIYUN.COM)
TRAVEL	LY (LY.COM)	FLIGGY (ALITRIP.COM)
BIKE SHARING	MOBIKE (MOBIKE.COM.CN)	OFO (OFO.SO)
ENTERPRISE PRODUCTIVITY	WECHAT ENTERPRISE, TIM (OFFICE.QQ.COM)	DINGTALK (DINGTALK.COM)
MAPS	TENCENT MAPS (MAP.QQ.COM)	AUTONAVI (DITU.AMAP.COM)
BANKING	WEBANK (WEBANK.COM)	MY BANK (MYBANK.CN)
O2O ON-DEMAND	MEITUAN DIANPING (MEITUAN.COM, DIANPING.COM)	KOUBEI / ELEME (KOUBEI.COM, ELE.ME)

Infographic courtesy of China Channel

4. **WeChat Pay**

Given that Chinese consumers are accustomed to mobile payments, companies operating in China need to support mobile payment methods for their virtual and physical stores. Taking into account the growing popularity of WeChat Pay, incorporating it has become a must.

5. **Wi-Fi Through WeChat**

This special WeChat feature can be activated by merchants and brands that own physical stores and hold official WeChat accounts. It can be accessed through a company's onsite services, usually at the top of the WeChat interface. Users must follow the brand's official account in order to connect with Wi-Fi. This way, offline users are attracted at zero cost, while merchants can get valuable user data.

Companies Engaging in Cross-Border E-Commerce

This company type sells their products through suppliers and international retailers. They have not officially entered China yet and use an intermediary business entity or online sales outlets in China. It is more useful for them to engage KOLs for their initial promotions than setting up official accounts on large platforms.

WeChat Articles on a KOL's Official Account

It is common to hire the services of KOLs to help newcomer brands gain recognition with Chinese consumers and test their product offerings before committing to a larger investment. KOLs contribute comprehensive articles, introducing the brand through product reviews and recommendations. Links to major online sales platforms or a flagship store already set up by the brand should be included in these articles.

WeChat Stores and the Coupons and Cards Feature

Brands can choose to offer only specific products for sale on a KOL's WeChat store. Some KOL WeChat stores offer a range of overseas products. Customers can buy onsite and receive product updates at the same time. Coupons and vouchers can also be distributed to boost sales.

Official Accounts and WeChat Articles

After the brand has gained some customers, they can open an official account and begin posting regular and relevant content to further promote their products or services.

Overseas Brands Serving Chinese Customers

These companies are physically located outside China. Their aim is not to sell their products to consumers living in Mainland China. Instead, their goal is to attract Chinese tourists and visitors and convince them to use their services when they travel abroad. Such brands often operate in the hospitality industry and include hotels, restaurants, or even private education institutions that want to attract international students from China. Such brands are likely unknown to the average Chinese consumer, and their biggest challenge is to stand out and get noticed by Chinese travelers.

Official Account

Holding an official account is a prerequisite to take advantage of most of the features described earlier. Therefore, these brands need to register for one. Outbound Chinese travelers use Weixin. Always remember the difference between Weixin and WeChat's international version explained earlier. Otherwise, you will never reach your target audience.

Overseas Moments Ads

Since 2017, WeChat allows overseas brands to launch Moments ads in specific regions or countries. Note that, as it is still at the open beta stage, it is not available to everyone. It is only available in certain regions. This feature allows companies and merchants located overseas to access outbound Chinese travelers or Chinese expatriates living abroad. Overseas Moments ads target users that log in to WeChat in a specific region or country. So far, however, no city-level targeting is available. At the time of printing, WeChat overseas advertising was open for 16 countries and regions including Taiwan, Macau, Hong Kong, Korea, Japan, Singapore, Malaysia, Thailand, Australia, the United States, Canada, New Zealand,

France, Germany, Italy, and the United Kingdom. The minimum budget varies based on the target country and region and also depends on the ad format.

The *Coupons and Cards* Feature

Overseas brands can give away digital vouchers and coupons through WeChat Shake or articles. Users can turn on their phone's Bluetooth, open WeChat Shake, and choose *Nearby*. They can shake their device to receive vouchers, coupons, and other special offers from nearby stores. Coupons must have wide validity dates so that users can collect them before their trip and use them overseas later. This feature is also a great way to drive traffic to offline merchants and businesses, especially hotels, restaurants, and retail stores.

WeChat Pay

WeChat Pay has conquered China and is now expanding to a number of overseas regions and countries. With the number of outbound Chinese tourists increasing rapidly, it has become a rigid demand for overseas merchants to support Chinese digital payment methods in order to offer convenience, address customers' needs, and encourage Chinese customers to spend more. WeChat Pay accounts can now be linked to foreign credit cards in Hong Kong, Taiwan, and Macao, and this can also be done by foreigners living in Mainland China. The major advantage of enabling WeChat Pay is that outbound Chinese visitors can shop overseas in RMB, based on real-time exchange rates, while WeChat Pay settles each transaction with overseas merchants based on local currency prices. Transactions can also be made in U.S. dollars. Major foreign currencies so far include, but are not limited to, USD, EUR, HKD, JPY, GBP, CAD, AUD, NZD, KRW, and so on.

WeChat Main Functions: Connect and Share

WeChat users can send messages, text, voice message, pictures, or videos to their contacts and groups. They can also make audio or video calls.

Link from other apps (QQ music, Weibo, Zhihu, and so on) can also be shared with WeChat friends either directly or through a group chat.

WeChat Shake

This particularly interesting and fun feature allows users to connect with others by shaking their phones at the same time. After that, they can add each other as friends and chat. Offline merchants like hotels and super-markets can also use WeChat Shake to make special offers. When users arrive at a designated location, they can open WeChat and shake their phones to get red envelopes, promotional codes, or coupons. TV stations have widely used this function to attract audiences and interact with them on a real-time basis. When people watch a TV program, the WeChat Shake logo often appears at the corner of the TV screen to remind view-ers to open WeChat and shake for red envelopes, gifts, lucky draws, or special offers.

People Nearby

Just as its name implies, this function helps people find other users nearby. They can then add each other as friends and chat if they are looking for friends or someone to date. This function works based on users' real-time location.

Moments

Moments is a major social networking function within WeChat. For gen-eral users, it works as a semi-closed platform where they can share all types of content: text, pictures, videos, articles, and even external links. These posts can only be seen by selected users. Moments is also a significant channel for brands to promote themselves and increase their follower base through ads and other types of content.

WeChat for Business Communication

WeChat is widely used at the workplace and has developed a number of features, such as easy file sharing and conference calling options, to streamline it for work. As a result, it is widely used for intranet communication. Enterprise accounts are used more and more for things like applying for leave, tracking projects, and submitting reimbursement forms. As most Chinese users use WeChat heavily anyway, it saves everyone's time and money. It is also increasingly common for colleagues and business professionals to scan each other's WeChat QR codes instead of exchanging business cards.

Digital Wallet

WeChat Wallet: Red Envelopes and Paying Bills

Red envelopes with lucky money are a Chinese tradition on special occasions, but they have now evolved into a digital form. Now with WeChat, red packets can be offered with one's WeChat Wallet balance or through account-linked bank cards. WeChat Wallet can also be used to settle bills by scanning a QR code or having one's own QR codes scanned by merchants. Users can also transfer money directly to each other easily. There is even a *Go Dutch* function that makes it easier to pay for group activities such as team lunches.

Third-party Applications and Mini Programs

WeChat is also a platform for third-party applications, and there are mini programs for services such as paying for taxi services, shared bikes, paying utility bills, and much more. Mini programs even allow users to shop online, so they do not have to leave WeChat to use online shopping websites or applications. Third-party applications for booking flights and hotels also work within the app.

A Finger on the Pulse

Official Accounts

A variety of official accounts established by brands, media, or even individuals are available for users to subscribe to. They produce articles, news, stories, product reviews, and more. They update daily, so people can get a lot of information through official account subscriptions.

WeChat has announced that, in the near future, they will be launching a special app for official accounts that is expected to provide expanded marketing opportunities for brands.

Information Mini Programs

If users have already a favorite magazine or newspaper, they can check for their mini program so that they can receive regular updates without leaving WeChat or switching to other media sources.

Search

Now that WeChat is improving its search function, information is becoming easier to find. You can search for any type of content such as articles published by official accounts, mini programs, content published by friends and fellow group members, conversation history, stickers, and so forth. Users can also do research on products they want to buy or find news on certain topics from the media, the public, and their friends, all within WeChat.

Necessary Steps to an Effective Social Marketing Campaign

- Your company's social media pages should be updated on a weekly, if not daily basis. Make sure that your posts link back to your company's website to drive more traffic.
- Direct communication is a key element for an effective digital marketing campaign targeting Chinese users. Make sure that you use social media platforms in a way that inspires dialogue in order to keep your followers engaged.
- Interested customers should be given available options for directly asking questions related to your product or service. Make sure your response to inquiries is always prompt and personal.
- It is crucial that you understand fully the needs and preferences of your targeted consumers. This will allow you to tailor your offering to local tastes, and it is a necessary step to building a unique value proposition.

How to Market on Weibo

As an information-driven platform, Weibo spreads quickly and widely. Users get the latest news and information on the platform, voice their own opinions, and start discussions with fellow netizens. Most users come to Weibo for interesting and funny multimedia content. They discuss about current events, personal interests, celebrity gossip, movies, and TV dramas. Heated discussions often become hot topics on Weibo. Brands usually integrate positive and funny trending issues in their copywriting in order to gain additional exposure. Weibo users currently prefer multimedia content, with short videos being the most popular content type. Weibo Story—which streams 15-second short videos and photos in a slideshow format—has witnessed remarkable growth among Weibo users. Users enjoy watching all kinds of live streaming on Weibo, like brand special events, celebrity interviews, and so on.

Weibo's Working Model

Weibo is one of China's leading social media platforms to discuss about personal interests, latest news, and celebrity gossip. It has a simple working model with entertainment at its core. In 2009, before WeChat's launch by Tencent, Weibo's first batch of users could mainly update their status and connect with friends on the platform. Users became addicted, and this phase lasted for quite some time. An increasing number of media outlets and celebrities opened accounts, and many people started following them, boosting the platform. After this first phase, users started using Weibo as a self-broadcasting tool. They uploaded photos and wrote posts to reflect aspects of their personality. They connected with users with similar interests for a sense of belonging and recognition. The funny, beautiful, knowledgeable, and professional began to emerge out of this crowded scene, and with time, some of them became popular. Those with the ambition and foresight to increase and strengthen their fame won in the end, and this trend expanded Weibo's scope well beyond that of a merely social networking platform.

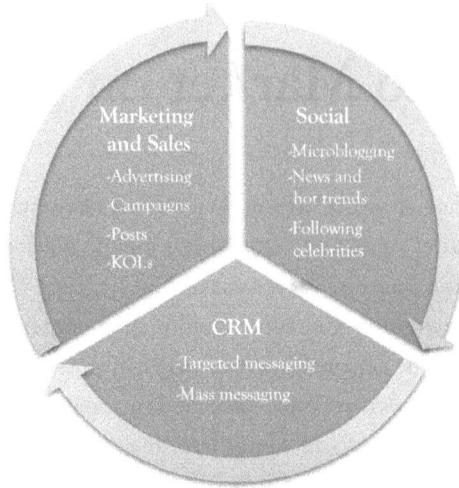

User Demographics

The majority of Weibo's monthly active users are under the age of 30 years, and they represent 80 percent of the platform's total monthly active users. They are also well-educated, with 77.8 percent holding a bachelor's degree or higher. Half of Weibo's monthly users come from third- and fourth-tier cities. Male users (56.3 percent) outnumber female users (43.7 percent). Weibo's stated goal is to become China's national social platform. The great majority of users (92 percent) access Weibo through its mobile app. They are interested in entertainment-related topics, such as dining out, music, sports, movies, and celebrities. Each user follows on average 200 official accounts, while every five minutes, a new post appears in their stream.

Marketing and Advertising

As a public, open platform, Weibo has evolved into a very powerful digital promotion tool. Once qualified merchants and brands set up their official account, they can launch all sorts of marketing and paid advertising campaigns. Topic hashtags, feed recommendations, and the search function help brands reach potential customers with their campaign posts. In fact, it is far easier to gain popularity and increase one's follower base on Weibo than it is on WeChat. In addition to traditional advertising and campaigns, brands use paid product placements and brand ambassadors with Weibo celebrities to attract more followers. Formal, monetarily compensated agreements are entered into with influential bloggers and KOLs operating on Weibo. Unlike the West, it still not a requirement for KOLs to declare these arrangements or to label sponsored content. A big number of brands and independent merchants prefer this type of promotion, as it is less expensive and allows them to reach large audiences, which generally results into a higher conversion rate.

Sales

Weibo cooperates with Taobao and Tmall to facilitate sales on their platform. They have worked together with Alibaba to launch the Weibo Window, a function for direct sales. Alibaba, which owns Taobao and Tmall, became a Weibo shareholder in early 2013. Back then, Alibaba held an 18 percent stake in Weibo, which by March 2017, rose to 31 percent. Weibo Window allows both Taobao individual sellers and brands having their official stores on Tmall to import product links from these two platforms and sell their products without switching between platforms. In addition, the Weibo Wallet function offers users the possibility to sell directly on Weibo. Its popularity is, however, far lower compared to WeChat Wallet.

CRM

Weibo can also be a valuable CRM tool. The platform provides basic customer service functions like custom menu bars and mass messaging. Users can get information by sending messages to a brand's account or by simply using the keyword autoreply function in the menu bar. Brands should make full use of these standard features to maintain a communication channel with their customers.

How to Market on Weibo

With a large audience and high penetration rates, Weibo is one of the most effective marketing tools for businesses to engage with existing and potential customers. However, building a quality Weibo account is not easy, as it requires time, effort, and most importantly, the right marketing strategies.

Weibo Accounts

There are two main types of Weibo accounts: personal and corporate accounts. A personal account is for individual users, while corporate accounts are for organizations, companies, businesses, and media. There is no registration fee required for setting up these two types of accounts. Once you have set up a regular corporate account, you need to follow the necessary steps to get it verified. Verified accounts are indicated by a blue or orange *V*. They offer their users additional privileges and marketing features, and they indicate they are legitimate. It is important to know that different verification procedures are required for personal and corporate accounts.

Personal Accounts

Verifying a personal account is fairly simple for someone based in Mainland China. All you will need is a local mobile phone number to link to the account and a face photograph in digital format. Note that only active accounts with more than 100 followers that follow more than 30 accounts can be verified. On top of this, you are required to have at least two friends with verified personal accounts. If you do not reside in China and you would like to have your personal account verified, you need to provide more documentation, including proof of employment, business cards, proof of identity such as your passport or driver's license, as well as a certification in an industry that is relevant to your account.

Corporate Accounts

Verifying the corporate account of a China-registered company requires that the company submit their Chinese business license, an application letter, contact details of the account administrator, and a verification fee of 300 RMB. If, however, your company is outside China, you will need to submit an application letter, third-party authorization letter, company registration documents with a certified translation in Mandarin Chinese, contact details of your account administrator, and a verification fee of 1,000 U.S. dollars. While for overseas account verification, you can submit all necessary documents by yourself; it is best to hire a local agency to prepare and submit all required documents. Once a personal account is verified, an orange *V* is displayed next to the account holder's profile picture, while a blue *V* is displayed next to the company's logo on verified corporate accounts. Both types of accounts can launch campaigns through the activity center. Verified corporate accounts can pin posts, change their cover picture, and add up to five images in the slideshow section. Once you have your account verified, you are ready to start your marketing activities.

Posting Frequency

There are about 100 million messages posted on Weibo. With such a fierce competition, your account's posting frequency is very important. To catch your followers' attention and make them remember you, you need to be very consistent and post on a very regular basis. For most official accounts, it is common practice to publish at least one post per day. Large brands generally have a higher posting frequency of three to five posts per day. Many bloggers and Weibo KOLs even broadcast every few hours. If you have just set up your Weibo account, two or three daily posts are highly recommended to build initial content for your visitors.

Content Types

International brands often make their accounts look very much like a commercial, by constantly posting beautiful pictures of their products. Weibo is, however, the place where people look for engagement and entertainment. Content needs to be diversified; it needs to be a mix of informing, entertaining, interacting, and promoting in equal measure, if you want to keep your followers engaged. Your content must reflect your understanding of trending topics and current styles. Positioning should transmit meaningful values and knowledge to the readers. It is important that you build a content plan for both your WeChat and Weibo accounts. In the next section, you can see a few content categories.

Trending Topics

Such topics can be related to anything. A noteworthy event in the news, a recent film or book release, a festival, special occasions, and more. Hashtags and trending topics can be easily found on Weibo's search page. However, these topics change rapidly from hour to hour, so it is important that you stay tuned. It is imperative that you seize the opportunity and write a post right away, whenever you spot a popular topic that is related to your product or industry.

Practical Tips

Practical tips are an all-time classic! They are one of the most popular types of content on Weibo, enjoy a higher engagement, and tend to be shared more often. You can write informative posts and articles and educate your followers on specific topics that are related to your industry and expertise. For instance, a soft way of promotion includes giving instructions on how customers can make best use of your products.

Funny Posts

Adding humor to your posts is another way to catch readers' attention. Witty posts appeal to audiences' positive emotions and help them remember your brand. This approach could be less appropriate for highly regulated industries, such as finance and health care.

Interactive Posts

Combining social media and interactive content is a great way to trigger discussion and drive traffic. You can interact with your followers by asking questions, collecting their opinions on specific topics, inviting them to participate in polls, and so on. This kind of interactive content, however, should be posted only after the account has a sufficient follower base or there will not be much interaction.

Brand-Related Content

Your topics can also revolve around your brand, your team's projects, corporate achievements, and most importantly, your products and their unique features. Brands can also update their followers on recent events and product launches. Sharing user reviews and industry news is a great way to showcase credibility.

Sales

Showcasing products is an effective way to increase visibility and sales conversions. Whenever you launch a special offer, make an announcement to notify your followers. You can also give away some exclusive trial products to your followers to generate buzz and excitement and to also collect feedback.

Additional features to make content stand out include visuals such as videos, images, and GIFs. Visuals are key to catch viewers' attention. Whenever possible, add rich media to your posts and articles, such as images, emoticons, and videos.

Videos

Videos can be directly uploaded to Weibo or reposted from other applications and websites. Weibo supports major video formats and allows URLs from other video sites, including Youku, Tudou, Sina Broadcast, Sohu, Qiyi, LeTV, and Yinyuetai.

Images

Each Weibo post can accommodate up to nine images. If you have gathered enough visual material or employ an in-house designer, try to use nine pictures at once. They will be displayed in a nice 3 × 3 grid and have an eye-catching effect. A combination of 3, 4, or 6 pictures also displays nicely on both mobile interfaces and desktops.

GIFs

GIFs are animated images. They are very popular on social media because they offer a wordless, clear, and funny way to express an idea, communicate a joke, or tell a story. GIFs are a great tool for product introductions. Instead of overwhelming readers with text, you can describe your product's features and demonstrate them through a GIF collection.

In sum:

- Positive and humorous posts can be very successful when they are closely related to a hot topic, your brand, and your target consumers or audience.
- Content types must be mixed masterfully to achieve synergy. For example, sales promotion posts must also be interactive, fun, and informative in some way to engage followers.
- Ask your team and all company staff—do not limit promotion to the marketing team—to regularly share brand-related content on Weibo. It is common for employees to promote their company's product in China.
- Post frequency is key to maintaining your account's strength. Established brands need to post three to eight times a day, especially retail companies.
- Brands need to live stream and post short videos at least once a week. Use Weibo's catchy emoticons and use GIFs to make your posts stand out.

Weibo Advertising

Due to Weibo's increasing popularity, marketers are flocking to the platform for online brand advertising. Advertising on Weibo has always been Sina's major source of revenue. Compared with WeChat, Weibo offers more targeted and diverse advertising options for brands to increase exposure and reach out to focused market demographics. The four major advertising options are display ads, Weibo search engine promotion, fan tunnel, and fan headlines. Brands need to tailor a distinct strategy for each of each type. A combined approach naturally works best.

Display Ads

Also, known under the term *banner ads*, they are featured on the Weibo homepage, on the side of users' newsfeed, and on the search page of the *Discover* section. Marketers can choose various ad sizes and placements across the Web and mobile versions. You can select keywords to control their visibility based on user searches and have them displayed on relevant accounts. All these parameters determine the final cost. When a user clicks on the display ad, they are directed to the brand's landing page. So, they are very effective for driving traffic to an external link. Display ads are great for promoting events and launching sales campaigns.

Fan Headlines

This type of advertising is most useful for boosting posts to existing followers, increase exposure, and enhance fan engagement. Boosted posts feature a *promoted* tag, but keep the format of regular posts. The price of each promotion depends on the number of followers. The bigger the number, the more expensive it is.

Fan Tunnel

Fan tunnel is a more targeted way for brands to increase their follower base and reach out to their target audience. It offers more targeting options for them to promote posts on their Weibo account. You can define the target audience by specifying your criteria based on region, age, gender, interests, and even, device types. You can also target followers of other accounts or similar niches. Fan tunnel promotion costs are typically calculated in CPM and pricing starts from five RMB per 1,000 views.

Weibo Campaigns

Launching campaigns is a part of Weibo marketing. Not only can they bring you new followers, but also keep your existing followers engaged.

In general, Weibo users love participating in all sorts of campaigns for fun and to win prizes. There are two major types of campaigns on Weibo: system campaigns and creative campaigns. System campaigns have basic formats and rules defined by Weibo. They can be only launched by verified corporate accounts. Creative campaigns are created and customized according to the organizer's goals and needs. They can be launched by all accounts. Launching a Weibo campaign is free, so you only need to allocate budget for promotion and prizes. Eye-catching visual designs and easy, fun participation formats are the best ingredients for any successful Weibo campaign.

System Campaigns

To launch a system campaign, the account administrator must go to the activity center in the management center to set up and submit the campaign details. Once the campaign is approved, it will be launched on the scheduled day. There are six types of system campaigns that Weibo offers.

Free Trial Campaigns

This type of campaign allows brands to distribute products or product samples to your target audience when you release a new product. To get prizes and gifts, users give reasons why they should be selected. Finally, at the end of the campaign, brands can pick the winners based on the content quality of their posts, while at the same time, they can collect useful market feedback on the advertised products.

Content Collection Campaign

This campaign format encourages users to contribute original content related to a specific topic. The format includes videos, pictures, reviews, or slogans. At the end of the campaign, brands pick the winners based on the quality of content.

Repost Campaign

This requires that users repost a designated post. As the campaign organizer, you can also decide whether users need to follow your account or tag a few friends in the repost message. At the end of the campaign, winners are randomly selected by the system.

Pre-Ordering Campaign

Pre-ordering campaigns are a great way to draw attention and create buzz before an official product release. This campaign format allows users to pre-order products before they are launched. At the end of the campaign, only users who have participated can purchase the products. It appears that purchase links must be connected to Alibaba, or they will be difficult to post.

Lucky Roulette Campaign

This type of campaign allows users to spin a roulette wheel for a chance to win a prize immediately. You can offer a wide range of prizes in this campaign.

Flash Sales Campaign

This is very similar to a Lucky Roulette campaign, but it suits best e-commerce and O2O businesses. Users can win gifts or receive special discounts for promoted products and for a limited time period.

Creative Campaigns

Creative campaigns allow the administrator to design the format and rules of their campaign. Creative campaigns are generally created as a post clearly stating the campaign period, prizes, number of winners, participation procedures, and other terms and conditions. At the end of each campaign, you can either handpick the winners by yourself or use a third-party application to select winners who followed the campaign rules. By using this add-on, winners will be notified by automatic private message to submit their contact details, so that the brand can send the prize they won.

How to Sell on Weibo

One of the easiest ways to sell your products on Weibo is to insert a purchase link in your article or promotional post. This is the most widespread form of social media monetization in China. Given that Alibaba holds a 31.5 percent stake in Weibo, and it seems to have introduced a process to block links to sites that are not Alibaba properties, brands need to set up an outlet on Taobao, Tmall, Aliexpress, or Alibaba before starting this phase. In early 2015, Weibo in cooperation with two mainstream e-commerce platforms, Jumei and Taobao, launched Weibo Window. The total number of Weibo Window users exceeded 1.3 million, and its daily exposures reached 180 million.

Weibo Window

Weibo Window is an e-commerce feature that allows users to set up mini stores on their Weibo accounts. These online stores are native to Weibo, and they link to other Alibaba marketplaces. Weibo Window is open to all users. Under the tab *Weibo Window* in the management center, you can add products for sale. When uploading the product information, the administrator needs to input the purchase links to Jumei, Taobao, and Tmall to complete this part of the process. Product information can be edited further before publishing. Once this information is published, a new Weibo Window section is added to the brand's page, below their name or company card. Other users can check out the brand's product list, make purchases, and read product reviews.

Weibo Window Product Cards

Aside from adding products to Weibo Window, you can create promotional posts using the product card feature. If you are using a desktop version, you need to insert the URL of the product from Weibo Window, and the post will automatically showcase the product card. If you are using the mobile application, you need to create the post by selecting the *Product* option. You may select any product in the Weibo Window section and create a post to promote it. A promoted post is similar to a regular one, but with a product card below it. The product card includes the product image, product details, and price. Users can click on it to know more about the product and to purchase it. In addition, product cards can be also inserted into long articles. A long article that introduces your product with a featured product card can be a great form of soft promotion. You can add up to 20 product cards in each article. Next are listed some recommendations you can follow when creating posts featuring product cards:

- Add personalized images or videos in your promotional post to attract attention.
- Launch giveaway campaigns to stimulate interaction and sharing of your posts.
- Make sure you attach the hashtag #WeiboWindow# or other hot hashtags to increase exposure and make your post more searchable on Weibo.
- Encourage your customers to share their purchases on Weibo to increase.

Weibo as a Customer Relationship Management Tool

As Weibo is an open platform for sharing and discussion, it is important that brands make the most out of the features and possibilities it offers. Weibo is a great tool for sending welcome messages to new followers, replying to messages and comments, interacting with other Weibo-related accounts, even managing a crisis. Brands need to communicate and interact with their followers in a proactive and personalized fashion. Quality interactions will help increase your fan loyalty, boost likes, shares, and conversions. Verified Weibo accounts send automatic welcome messages to users once they follow the brand's account. The default message is in Chinese and can be translated to *Thank you for following our account.* Brands can, however, customize their welcome message for 5,000 RMB. A customized welcome message should include a company introduction, detail what users can expect of the account, and have a call to action. Do not forget to share information and links of your presence on other social media platforms and cross-promote.

To build a close relationship with your followers, be personable, friendly, and promptly reply to as many comments as possible. Be genuine and sincere when dealing with customer issues. Make sure you show appreciation when receiving positive reviews and recommendations. When you receive negative reviews and comments, always address the issue clearly and apologize when necessary. For complicated issues, have your customer support team contact the customer to discuss the problem.

Every time users mention and tag your brand on Weibo, you will receive a system notification. There are tons of official accounts on Weibo, and you can easily find other accounts in the same industry. Follow industry-related accounts to assert your presence and build relationships with them. You can also engage with other industry players on Weibo and comment on their own posts. No celebrity or brand is immune to negative comments and complaints. When a crisis arises, address the issue in a professional and timely manner. It is important to not dwell on this situation too long, remain positive and do remember that bad media is often better than no media at all.

Weibo crisis management tips:

- To respond quickly to any crisis, assign a full-time staff member or hire an agency to monitor and manage your Weibo account.
- Do not delete negative comments, unless, of course, if they are spam. To rebuild trust and loyalty, it is important to empathize with the customer and be straightforward on how you plan to resolve the issue. Always apologize for any inconvenience caused.
- Always release an official Weibo statement after a crisis has occurred. Publish the statement on the company's website and other social media, so that everyone becomes aware.
- After the crisis, thank customers and users for their patience with another official statement. Tell users what you have learned from this crisis and what measures you have taken to prevent a similar issue from happening again in the future. The ultimate goal is to make your customers feel confident in your brand again.

Zombie Fans and Fake Accounts

Fake accounts and bots are flourishing everywhere on social media, and Weibo is no exception. Fake accounts—also known as *zombie followers*—refer to accounts that are not created or managed by real users. They are not completely *dead*, however, as they can still follow other accounts, like, comment and repost. Many brands and KOLs often buy zombie followers to boost their fan base and make their account appear more popular. Zombie followers can be generated using a special software or can be simply bought online. For example, you can find many providers selling zombie followers on Taobao and other platforms for as little as one U.S. dollar for 1,000 followers. Fake followers come in a various qualities. For high-quality ones, users can define parameters such as nationality, gender, and geographic location in order to make their look more *real*.

By the same logic, fake interactions such as comments, likes, reposts can also be bought. Some brands buy them in order to increase their account's amount of interactions so they can look more popular and show that they enjoy a high engagement rate. Very often, they are used to meet marketing KPIs (key performance indicators). It is interesting to notice that the term used in China to describe zombie followers is *wangluo shuijun*, which can be translated as *Internet water army*. Many Chinese companies—and often government agencies—employ them to post on social media to influence public opinion. Buying zombie followers and fake interactions does not bring actual value, and very often, is a waste of resources. Weibo regularly conducts cleanup campaigns on inactive accounts in order to provide a clean environment and a more accurate assessment of brands' popularity. Very often, accounts buying zombie followers experience a sudden and significant drop in their number of followers, and in some cases, these accounts end up being deactivated by Weibo. Accounts that buy fake followers can also ruin their company's reputation and credibility. People can easily spot fake accounts, and users are naturally turned off when they find brands following such tactics.

In any case, it is important to be aware that there are thousands of zombie followers on Weibo. Paying for zombie followers is against Weibo's ethics and regulations. When hiring KOLs to promote your brand, understand that they may have purchased zombie accounts and interactions.

The Future of Weibo

Weibo is an ideal platform for marketing and advertising, primarily thanks to its open and public nature. It allows brands to establish a strong brand image, grow initial followers, and develop new relationships. Different types of Weibo ads and the platform's search engine ensure a higher exposure than WeChat, at least at the initial stage. One of Weibo's major advantages is that it provides excellent opportunities for brands to do hot topic marketing and gain further exposure. The downside is that negative news also spreads quickly when, for example, a PR crisis hits the brand. In the first part of the book, three types of companies were discussed based on their China entry strategy. The first category includes international brands that are already established in China, the second brand doing cross-border e-commerce, and finally, overseas companies serving Chinese outbound travelers. In this section, we will see how these three different types of companies can use Weibo and which are the most relevant tools and features for each company type.

1. **International Brands Already Established in China**
   This term refers to brands that have already established a legal entity in China. They own physical and/or online stores in Mainland China. They employ local staff and are familiar with the local e-commerce ecosystem. These brands are known by some Chinese consumers.

Official Account and Weibo Wall

International brands usually have an official Weibo account and an official WeChat account. They manage both at the same time as part of a combined social media strategy. This not only ensures consistency in terms of content on both platforms, but also drives followers from one platform to the other, thus expanding their influence. Regular posts are essential to keeping the audience engaged, but be aware that Weibo posts are much shorter than on other platforms. Finding a suitable language style, publishing diversified content, and maintaining a regular posting rhythm are key. Your Weibo brand account must be filled with diversified and informative multimedia content. An official account enables brands to launch different types of marketing campaigns. It is an effective way to gain exposure, grow followers, and boost interaction on the platform.

Weibo Customer Service

Although Weibo is not designed as a platform for CRM, the mass messaging function and the custom menu bar in the private message dialog box still play a crucial role in customer service. Pre- and after-sales questions can be quickly answered in a fast and straightforward fashion. It is best when brands get first-hand feedback from customers on their products.

Weibo Window

Weibo's cooperation with Alibaba has led to the creation of Weibo Window. Brands with official Tmall stores and individual Taobao merchants can import product links from these two platforms and sell directly on Weibo. They can even manage all their merchandise and orders on Weibo without leaving the platform.

1. **Brands Engaging in Cross-border E-commerce**
   These companies sell their products through international retailers and suppliers. They can set up a Weibo account, even without a China-based official legal entity. It is common practice for them to hire the services of KOLs for their initial product promotions.

Official Account and Weibo Wall

When brands have accumulated a good customer base, they are ready to open an official account and start posting regular content for further promotion.

KOL Weibo Posts

It is common to partner up Weibo KOLs to contribute to a comprehensive brand introduction. Product reviews, recommendations, comprehensive Weibo articles with links to Alibaba platforms where the brand has set up its official flagship store.

Weibo Window and KOLs

Another kind of KOL cooperation involves offering specific products for sale on the KOL's Taobao store. Many KOLs are individual sellers and offer a number of international brands and foreign products for sale. Weibo Window enables them to import product links for direct sale.

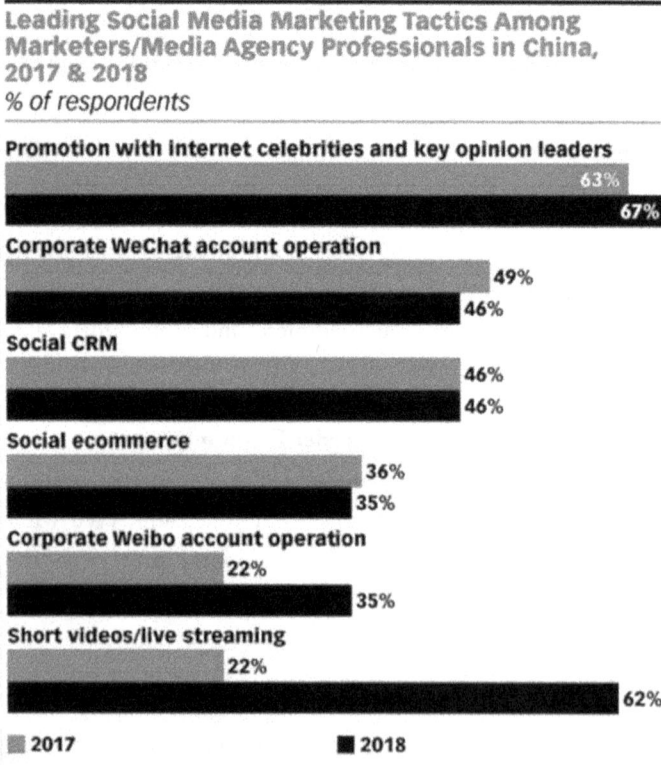

Leading Social Media Marketing Tactics Among Marketers/Media Agency Professionals in China, 2017 & 2018
% of respondents

Promotion with internet celebrities and key opinion leaders
- 63%
- 67%

Corporate WeChat account operation
- 49%
- 46%

Social CRM
- 46%
- 46%

Social ecommerce
- 36%
- 35%

Corporate Weibo account operation
- 22%
- 35%

Short videos/live streaming
- 22%
- 62%

■ 2017   ■ 2018

Source: AdMaster and top marketing. "2018 digital marketing trends report." January 3, 2018.

Note: 2017 n=93; 2018 n=90.

Overseas Brands Serving Outbound Chinese Travelers

Such companies are geographically located outside of China. Their goal is not to sell their products to China-based consumers, but instead, to attract Chinese travelers to buy their services and products abroad. These can be companies in the hospitality industry like hotels and restaurants or even, international private schools that want to attract international students from South East Asia.

Official Account and User-Generated Content Campaigns

An official account enables its holder to launch UGC campaigns. International brands can encourage their Chinese customers and followers to write short product reviews and/or upload beautiful pictures on Weibo while adding specific hashtags and mentioning the brand's official account.

Weibo Advertising

Search engine promotion, banner ads, landing page ads, fan tunnel ads are but a few of the advertising options offered by Weibo. Thanks to the platform's open and public nature, ads appear in followers' feeds and promise wide exposure. Usually, Weibo ads drive users to a specific landing page such as a campaign page, the brand's e-shop, or an official Weibo account. Therefore, it is best to launch a campaign at the same time. Offering coupons and discounts are a great way to attract more followers.

Live Streaming

Weibo has partnered with Yizhibo to offer its users a live stream experience. Live streaming allows users to enjoy a vivid and entertaining demonstration of a brand's products. Overseas brands can invite KOLs for free visits. They can host live streams to introduce their brand and showcase their services, products, and facilities. They can also launch lucky draw campaigns with special offers as prizes.

To sum up:

	Marketing strategies for WeChat and Weibo	
	WeChat	Weibo
Increase exposure	Interactive H5 KOL promotion UGC + incentives Unique content	Intensive ads KOL promotion Creative video Live streaming
Increase sales	WeChat ads KOL crossover Exclusive coupons + discounts	Campaigns + Weibo Window KOL promotional codes KOL trial Live streaming with *Watch and Buy*
Increase followers	Lucky draws UGC + incentives KOL promotion	Lucky draw UGC + incentives KOL live streaming

The Taobao Phenomenon: Can You Beat the Giant?

Taobao, a brand owned by the Alibaba Holdings group, which is also the owner of the B2B site Alibaba.com and Tmall, is the clear leader in China's e-tail landscape. It would not be an exaggeration to claim that the company has shaped the e-commerce landscape of the country. A very interesting fact that has been noticed on the 2016 Forbes list of 30 outstanding entrepreneurs under the age of 30 years in China is that a major common characteristic most of them share is their connection to Taobao. In reality, Taobao is the place where former factory workers and farmers get their first taste of entrepreneurship by setting up their online storefronts to sell all sorts of goods and services to China's rising consumer class. It is crucial for both local and foreign companies to understand at which point Taobao is defining their online presence. Many Western companies are totally unaware of how their products are already being sold on Taobao by other merchants or local distributors. Companies without a well-defined and focused online strategy are allowing a channel with a very rapid growth to develop without their influence or control.

Although in Western minds, Taobao is the counterpart of eBay in China, it is different from eBay, in that it does not primarily sell second-hand products. The great majority of items sold on Taobao are new. There are three main categories of merchants: microbusinesses, distributors who sell their excess inventory, and suppliers who cannot access other retail channels. The site boasts over one million online products, of which 50,000 are sold per minute. Shoppers maintain that products sold on Taobao cost on average 25 percent less than through other e-tail channels.

Taobao enjoys high consumer loyalty due to its bargain prices and convenience, as well as a number of other unique characteristics. One of its unique advantages is its enormous pool of e-merchants. Back in 2003, when it was first launched, the site was rather a latecomer in China's C2C market. Yet, within just two years, it managed to capture more than

60 percent of the market share, thanks to its very popular *no-fee strategy*. Taobao does not charge any registration or transaction fees. After its successful launch, the site took off higher through the network links it created: its large merchant pool led to a huge consumer traffic, which attracted even more sellers generating in turn more consumer traffic.

Shoppers seem to particularly appreciate Taobao's customer care service. The site has the biggest call center worldwide, and a very innovative instant messaging tool known as Taobao WangWang, which allows e-sellers to communicate with their customers in real time, 24/7. Amazingly enough, every shop on Taobao has two to three customer service representatives available online at any time. Another feature that is particularly valued by Chinese consumers is the site's seller credibility rating system that allows buyers to rate products and post feedback about sellers. This rating system helped build a high level of trust in the products sold. It generates comments by many customers and takes the shopping experience to a higher level by making it appealing, interactive, and social.

In another successful effort to diversify from its no-fee strategy, Alibaba restructured Taobao in 2011 into three distinct companies: Taobao Marketplace, eTao (a service for searching and comparing products across various Chinese e-commerce websites), and Tmall (Taobao Mall). This strategic move enabled them to offer consumers a more complete and sophisticated online shopping experience and gave each of the three companies more freedom for more strategic initiatives and future innovations. Tmall was launched in 2009. The platform mimics an offline mall offering various product categories on different virtual floors. They also offer storewide discounts, sales, as well as a loyalty points system. Tmall is more selective compared with the original Taobao and offers higher-quality customer service and reliability. Participating sellers and brands are charged registration and transaction fees and must be authenticated by Tmall. Many local and international branded suppliers already have their official virtual stores set on Tmall, directly or through licensed distributors. Tmall benefits from synergy with Taobao because searches on Taobao direct users to Tmall when appropriate.

New competitor sites have emerged in recent years, and although the user base of these new platforms is much smaller than Taobao and Tmall, some of them enjoy increasingly larger traffic. E-shoppers who have switched from Taobao to these sites perceive them as offering higher-quality products, better customer service, more flexibility, and faster shipping. These sites have higher prices, and their product selection is smaller than Taobao, but they attract consumers because their quality assurance is considered to be higher. B2C companies have seen a tremendous growth in categories that require high reliability and after-sales service, such as consumer electronics. Despite the success of these new websites, Taobao's dominant position will be difficult to shake in the foreseeable future, considering its increasingly large base of loyal customers. Taobao's market share is likely to decline in the future from the 80 percent share it enjoys currently, but it will nonetheless remain an important force in the e-commerce market.

China's Most Popular Search Engines

When it comes to e-commerce, the relationship between search engines and online retail websites is different in China compared with other markets. Generally, in other countries, any online search begins with Google. In China, the leading search engine is Baidu.com. However, Taobao has blocked the Baidu spider, which means that consumers cannot turn to Baidu search to find Taobao product listings. Instead, any search should start from within taobao.com. Considering that Taobao represents almost 80 percent of the total e-tail volume, Chinese e-shoppers do not rely on search engines as a way to find products online.

Online Marketing Practices That Will Not Work in China

A one-size-fits-all marketing strategy will not work in China. Social networks are a very effective way to engage with your online customers, but the rules and practices in China are different. A big challenge is the fragmentation of these social networks. There is no clear leader like Facebook in the West, but rather a multitude of social networks that attract different segments of users. For instance, Kaixin001.com attracts white-collar office crowds, Renren.com college students, Qzone appeals to young and active adults, and many other networks are aimed at other user segments.

Sina Weibo is an extremely popular microblogging network that is used by young professionals and celebrities. Widely used Western social networks such as Facebook and Twitter and popular websites such as YouTube are blocked within China. Google is also blocked, while Yahoo has a very limited number of users.

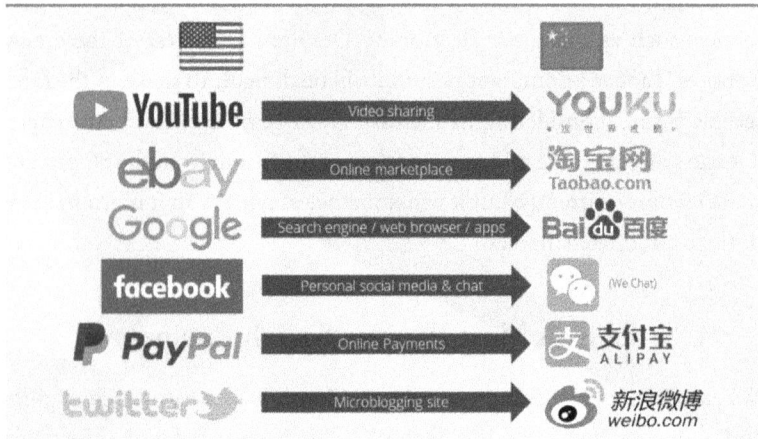

How Should Your Website Look to Attract Chinese Consumers?

Apart from creating a standalone website, there are several paths foreign companies can take when entering the Chinese e-tail market. In the event that a company chooses to create their independent website, there are a few things that they will have to take into account. It is imperative that your website's layout looks attractive to the average Chinese Internet user. Chinese websites differ from Western ones in terms of both content and layout. It is recommended that the website keeps some Western elements, such as simplicity and sophistication, while remaining attractive to Chinese users. Usability is another major issue to consider before designing your website. You need to make sure that it is user-friendly and fulfills the basic expectations of Chinese users. Chinese websites are typically more flashy and colorful. They contain larger amounts of information, more pictures, and more colors than Western websites. This phenomenon can be attributed to the fact that Chinese people are used to dealing fast with large amounts of information. According to another popular explanation, Chinese people would be *too lazy* to spend several minutes searching for information on a website; they expect to find all the information they need on the homepage. You also need to consider that Chinese netizens are constantly exposed to visual stimuli. Therefore, call-to-action buttons and other important information should look captivating and flashy if you want to attract their attention. Usability and a smart design are paramount in attracting and keeping customers. To satisfy Chinese e-shoppers, the website content should offer them possibilities for social interaction.

Chinese value face-to-face communication more than Western people. Considering the lack of personal communication in online shopping, consumer trust is harder to earn, in which case, a decent customer service available any time on the website becomes a necessity. In China, it is not common to send inquiry e-mails to ask for details on a product. Instant messaging is the most widely used way of communication. Online customer service should be as developed and sophisticated as possible and should be able to immediately address issues and questions that arise as users navigate the website. Chinese consumers are spoiled when it comes to online customer service. The minimum they expect is an efficient online chat service that will offer them the possibility to ask any questions they might have and get an answer within minutes or even seconds. Providing a full online service to your customers is crucial for success because failure to do so will automatically drive users to other websites where this service is provided. The process of choosing which product to buy has changed recently due to a system of Internet functions allowing customers to rate and review different aspects of the product and customer service. Chinese consumers regard product reviews as the most reliable source when deciding which product to purchase.

How to Sell Online

Operating a successful e-commerce portal will be a challenge for most foreign companies. A considerable amount of time and substantial investment will be required at the beginning. You might have to consider creating a website from scratch. Some other practical issues to take into account include website operating costs, handling of orders, and enquiries by e-mail, phone, or instant messenger, conducting inventory management, arranging shipments and package deliveries, and dealing with complaints and returns.

An ICP license is required for any foreign-invested company who wants to operate a standalone e-commerce website with a server based in China. However, the process of applying for an ICP license can be particularly time-consuming. This explains why it is mainly large multinational companies—equipped with vast resources and a strong brand image—that are the privileged owners of standalone e-commerce websites in China.

The good news is that platform websites are about to become increasingly specialized and now offer tailor-made services to attract online customers, thus saving companies the hassle of creating and operating a costly e-commerce website. In 2017, standalone websites accounted for 8 percent of the total online retail value. The number of standalone websites is expected to decrease in China in the coming years, along with their market share, as online shopping will be concentrated in popular platform websites such as Taobao.com or Tmall. There are four main ways foreign companies can sell online in China, all of which have their own advantages and disadvantages.

Selling Through a Standalone Website Outside China

When companies choose to sell their products or services to Chinese consumers through an existing website outside of China, they will need to upgrade their language settings and include Chinese in the offered language menu options. The website will need to be upgraded in order to accept payments from Chinese credit cards. In this scenario, it is assumed that the company's operations are based outside of China, in which case, deliveries of products are treated as imports into China. Apart from the cost of customizing the website so that Chinese consumers can access it and use it easily, companies should also consider that their customers will have to bear higher shipping fees (which might also include custom fees) and long delivery times. Another drawback is that it will be hard for the company to manage after-sales service from a distance. Given that websites outside of China cannot obtain an ICP license, they may be susceptible to being blocked by local authorities.

Selling Through a Standalone Website Based in China

The costs of creating and operating a standalone website with a server based in China are basically the same as in the case of a standalone website outside of China. Assuming that the company has its operations based in China, delivery and after-sales service are no longer a problem. Still, as already mentioned, it is necessary to have an ICP license if a company plans to set up a China-based website. According to Chinese digital laws, only legal entities are permitted to apply for the required ICP license. In this case, foreign companies have two main options: either set up a legal entity in China or find a local partner, either a distributor or an agent who can assist them with the website registration in China.

Selling Through a Third-party Platform Outside China

The cheapest option for a company is to sell through an international third-party platform such as Amazon. Even so, this option is not likely to be very successful, as these platforms are not popular among Chinese consumers, and the traffic is rather limited. Long delivery times and debit or credit card requirements will be additional limitations.

Selling Through a Third-party Platform Based in China

China-based third-party platforms such as Taobao.com or JD.com offer several advantages as foreign companies can benefit from existing traffic without having to invest time and money in China SEO (search engine optimization). Another advantage is that Chinese customers are already familiar with these platforms' functionality and interface.

Foreign companies will still have to become familiar with the administration of these websites, especially their review and ranking systems. An annual membership fee is required to set up an online storefront on platforms like Tmall. Annual fees have risen dramatically over the last couple of years.

With respect to technology, there are four basic points to keep in mind:

- A China-hosted website will provide optimum Internet speed and accessibility.
- Websites should be optimized for mobile platforms.
- It is recommended that you invest in website optimization through local sites to increase user traffic.
- You might need to consider setting up an in-built payment system software specific to China to make payments in RMB easier and faster.

E-Commerce Models: Pros and Cons

Strategy	Advantages	Disadvantages
Selling through a standalone website outside China	Chinese consumers: • Can access goods not available in China Foreign sellers: • Do not need to go through Chinese bureaucracy to obtain an ICP license • Do not need to create a standalone website, especially for Chinese consumers	Chinese consumers: • Trust not guaranteed • Slow delivery • High shipping fees and risk • No after service • May not have credit card Foreign sellers: • Higher IT maintenance cost • No targeted marketing • Need for an import agent • May be blocked by Chinese authorities without notice
Selling through a China-based stand-alone website	Chinese consumers: • Faster Delivery	Chinese consumers: Foreign sellers: • Trust less than third-party platforms

	Foreign sellers: • Can provide a targeted offering to Chinese consumers	• Need to customize the website to Chinese consumers standards • Need efforts to generate traffic and reach Chinese consumers • The website must be registered to a company established in China • IT maintenance costs
Selling through a third-party platform outside China	Chinese consumers: • Access goods not available in China Foreign sellers: • Low cost • Understand how the platform works	Chinese consumers: • Language • Might not have credit card • Slow delivery • Higher shipping fees and parcel risk • Custom fees • No after service Foreign sellers: • Difficult to target consumers
Selling through a third-party platform based in China	Chinese consumers: • More likely to trust • Easier and faster online payments • Faster delivery • After service Foreign sellers: • Low cost • Benefit from the existing traffic provided by the platform	Foreign sellers: • Language • Marketing • Company registration in China • Certification requirements

Alternative Solutions

Cross-Border E-Commerce

There are currently 11 Free Trade Zones in Shanghai, each named after the province or municipality they are located in. The first Free Trade Zone was established in Shanghai in 2013. Three more zones were added in 2015, then another seven Free Trade Zones (FTZs) were announced in 2017. While the first four FTZs were established in coastal areas, in close proximity to sea ports, the most recent ones are located inland, a move indicating the government's plan to develop the economy of these inland areas. The initial size of Shanghai's FTZ was 28.78 square kilometers and has since increased fourfold. It currently totals 120 square kilometers. When the city launched the zone a few years ago, local officials aimed to transform it into a mini Hong Kong, a place where businesses from around the world could freely carry out investments and conduct commodity trading without foreign exchange controls and customs regulations. The zone has introduced a new model encouraging the financial and service sector companies that are so vital to China's consumer economy. The Shanghai FTZ was created with four goals in mind:

- Transitioning to a more market-friendly regulatory environment
- Increasing the competitive edge
- Internationalizing the RMB
- Testing new reform strategies with the aim to duplicate them in other parts of the country

The Shanghai FTZ laid the foundation for FTZs nationwide. The zone has attracted many multinational companies and banks since its creation. Also, following the inauguration of the Shanghai FTZ, a cross-border e-commerce platform, Kuajingtong.com, was launched. The platform is supported by the Shanghai Customs Bureau, the Shanghai Entry-Exit

Inspection and Quarantine Bureau, and the State Administration of Foreign Exchange. It offers advantages in authentic product guarantees, competitive prices, transparent taxes, convenient logistics, and customer service. Doing business in Shanghai's FTZ means not only being exempt of tariffs (zero or minimal tariffs), but you can also freely convert Chinese renminbi to any foreign currency both in current and capital accounts, and also the interest rates of renminbi can be determined through markets.

From brand name clothes, to cosmetics and food, a great number of Chinese consumers are fond of foreign, high-quality products. While many shoppers made purchases through third-party websites or individual online vendors, some were still worried about the authenticity and lawfulness of the products they purchased. Seeing this gap as a market opportunity, the Shanghai FTZ launched the country's first cross-border e-commerce platform called *kuajingtong.com*. Kuajingtong claims that products sold on its platform are generally 30 percent cheaper than those in retail stores. Although it is difficult for the platform to beat individual vendors or Taobao sellers who can offer even lower prices, the company's CEO says that he is confident about Kuajingtong's competing strengths. He maintains that the platform can guarantee the authenticity of the products along with fast delivery, reasonable prices, after-sales service, and transparent taxes.

The strategy for achieving these goals is to sign agreements with payment, logistics, and retail companies while closing deals with major global e-commerce companies such as eBay and Amazon. Consumers still have to pay customs duties for their purchases, but they will be able to save money. The idea is that, compared with the traditional model, the products are already in the FTZ, so consumers only need to pay customs and mail duties, which reduces logistic costs. The government has recently announced that controls will be relaxed over foreign investment within the FTZ in fields such as training, telecommunications, entertainment, international shipping, performance brokerage, and credit investigation.

Development of Free Trade Zones in China

Evolution of China's FTZs and Focus Industries

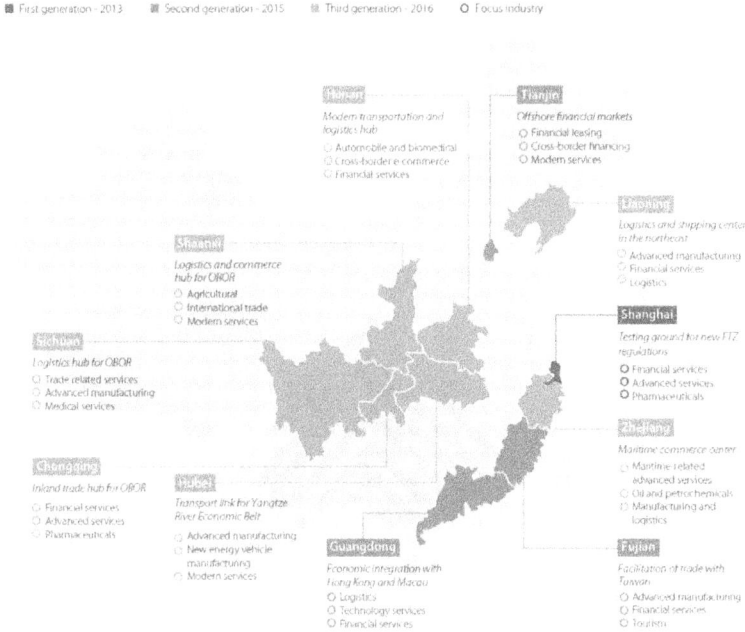

■ First generation - 2013   ■ Second generation - 2015   ▦ Third generation - 2016   ○ Focus industry

Hainan
Modern transportation and logistics hub
○ Automobile and biomedical
○ Cross-border e-commerce
○ Financial services

Tianjin
Offshore financial markets
○ Financial leasing
○ Cross-border financing
○ Modern services

Shaanxi
Logistics and commerce hub for OBOR
○ Agricultural
○ International trade
○ Modern services

Liaoning
Logistics and shipping centre in the northeast
○ Advanced manufacturing
○ Financial services
○ Logistics

Sichuan
Logistics hub for OBOR
○ Trade-related services
○ Advanced manufacturing
○ Medical services

Shanghai
Testing ground for new FTZ regulations
○ Financial services
○ Advanced services
○ Pharmaceuticals

Chongqing
Inland trade hub for OBOR
○ Financial services
○ Advanced services
○ Pharmaceuticals

Zhejiang
Maritime commerce center
○ Maritime related advanced services
○ Oil and petrochemicals
○ Manufacturing and logistics

Hubei
Transport link for Yangtze River Economic Belt
○ Advanced manufacturing
○ New energy vehicle manufacturing
○ Modern services

Guangdong
Economic integration with Hong Kong and Macao
○ Logistics
○ Technology services
○ Financial services

Fujian
Facilitation of trade with Taiwan
○ Advanced manufacturing
○ Financial services
○ Tourism

Total Number of FIEs and Registered Capital in FTZs*

■ Total number of FIEs   ■ Total registered capital (US$ billion)

	Shanghai	Fujian	Guangdong**	Tianjin
Total number of FIEs	17,304	2,799	6,366	3,375

FTZ* GDP Growth (2015 to 2016)

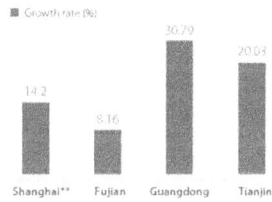

■ Growth rate (%)

Shanghai**	Fujian	Guangdong	Tianjin
14.2	8.16	30.79	20.03

* Seven new FTZs excluded due to unavailability of information; FIEs refer to foreign invested enterprises.
**Guangdong information available only until 2016.

*Seven new FTZs excluded due to unavailability of information.
**Data only represents Gross Industrial Product (GIP)

Graphic© Asia Briefing Ltd.

Courtesy of Asia Briefing Ltd.

Payment Methods

A couple of years ago, one of the most commonly cited obstacles to e-commerce penetration in China was the lack of effective methods of payment, especially considering the very limited credit card use at that time. Trying to deal with these issues and in an effort to win consumer confidence, Taobao introduced its Alipay escrow accounts system whereby customer payments are held in escrow until shoppers receive their orders. By contrast, PayPal, Alipay's Western counterpart, transfers the payment to the merchant automatically when the buyer places the order and merchants do not send out orders until payment is received. Alibaba created Alipay in 2004 to let millions of potential customers who lacked credit and debit cards shop on its vast online marketplace. Similarly, Tencent debuted its payments function in 2005 in a bid to keep users inside its messaging system longer. Alipay and WeChat have since become very popular, boasting one billion and 520 million monthly active users, respectively. Consumers sent more than three trillion U.S. dollars inside the two systems in 2017, equivalent to about half of all consumer goods sold in China during that year.

Key Payment Methods

China is a cash-oriented country. In everyday life, cash is by far the preferred way of payment because smaller companies and local shops do not always accept cards. New payment solutions have emerged in recent years as a result of booming e-commerce activities. The growth of e-commerce inspired the creation of new payment methods, such as Union Pay, which is the Chinese version of MasterCard or Visa, and Alipay, which is a third-party payment system that has been aforementioned. The explosive growth of e-commerce is largely due to the wide distribution and use of credit and debit cards in recent years, as well as the growth of third-party payment systems, such as Alipay and Tenpay, which have enabled consumers to feel more secure while carrying out online transactions. Online customers choose a variety of payment methods that are different from their counterparts in other countries. They prefer cash on delivery, wire transfers, online banking, and third-party online payment methods when shopping online. With regard to PayPal, although it is in theory permitted as a way of payment, it is still practically impossible to use a Chinese bank account for PayPal payments because Chinese banks are incompatible with this service. Another stumbling stone comes from the Chinese government's policy that consists in keeping a stable national currency by restricting cross-border transactions.

Cash on delivery (COD) remains a very popular payment method in China, especially in face-to-face transactions. However, while in 2012, almost 50 percent of the online consumers chose COD, this number decreased to 33 percent in 2013, then to 20 percent in 2018, at least when it comes to online shopping. Roughly, 75 percent of Chinese e-shoppers preferred online banking in 2017 as a way of payment for their online purchases, using both credit and debit card options. As for third-party online payment, it represents roughly 32 percent.

Online Banking Systems

The Bank of China was the first to introduce online payment gateway services in 1998 and was quickly followed by other major commercial banks. In fact, online banking systems were the main payment method in the initial stages of Chinese e-commerce. At that time, the lack of widely accepted standards offered banks the freedom to develop their own B2C e-banking services. They started offering online payment gateway services that allowed sellers to accept payments from customers' bank accounts. In the case that your company opts for this solution, it is important to know that, in order to set up the bank's payment system on their website, merchants need to download and install an application to establish communication with the issuer's gateway and also to identify themselves to the issuer. To settle payments, sellers need to open a settlement account with the issuing bank. This will require them to go to the bank and apply for the relevant online payment service. If your company wants to use several bank gateways to receive payments, the process will be time-consuming. The good news is that, with the expansion of Alipay and WeChat Pay, this method is becoming less and less popular.

Third-Party Payment Service Providers

Third-party platforms offer several practical advantages to foreign SMEs, mainly because they combine gateways of several Chinese and international banks. They function as middlemen between the seller and buyer, ensuring that customers will be satisfied with their purchases before any payment is remitted to the merchant. These platforms overcame one of the major drawbacks of e-commerce: consumer trust. Third-party payment is currently the most popular payment method in China. Third-party platforms offer a wide selection of card brands buyers can choose from before submitting their bank account number along with a password on the issuer's webpage.

An additional advantage of third-party payment methods is that they are easier to apply for and install on the company's Taobao or Tmall storefront. For instance, in the case of Alipay, installation is carried out by downloading and installing the required Alipay applications on the company's website. Alipay is by far the largest and most trusted third-party payment provider, and it is no surprise that China's e-tail industry really took off when Alipay introduced its services to the Chinese market.

Practically, it is a two-step settlement process: an interbank credit transfer takes place from the consumer's account to the provider's account, followed by a credit transfer from the provider's account to the seller's account. Typically, payments are settled periodically and not on a trade-by-trade basis. Alipay also launched a mobile wallet application, allowing users to make O2O payments.

Alipay charges fees based on the company's total annual transaction amount. Their sliding scale fees policy means that the larger the volume of your company's transactions, the lower the fee you pay.

Market share of leading third-party online payment providers in China, 2017

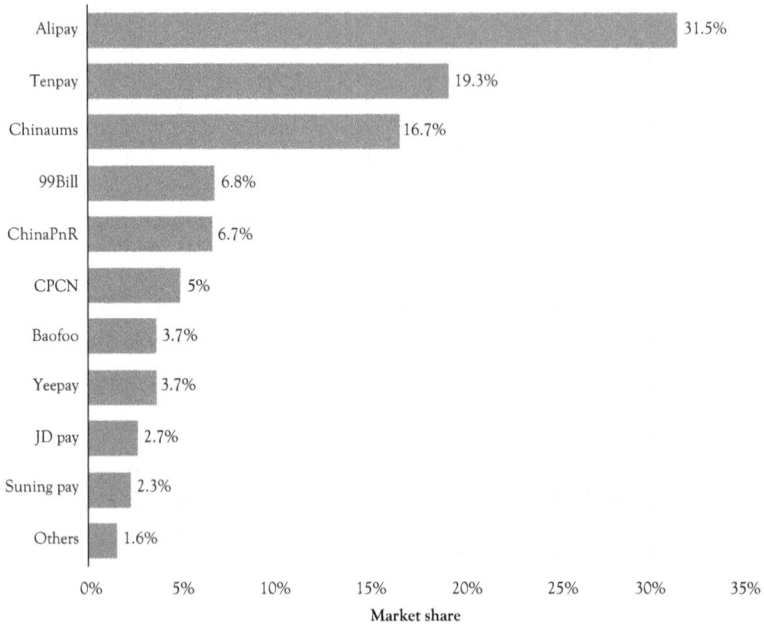

	Market share
Alipay	31.5%
Tenpay	19.3%
Chinaums	16.7%
99Bill	6.8%
ChinaPnR	6.7%
CPCN	5%
Baofoo	3.7%
Yeepay	3.7%
JD pay	2.7%
Suning pay	2.3%
Others	1.6%

Statista, Maverick China Research, company websites, 2017.

Cash or Payment on Delivery

Cash or POD is still among the most popular payment methods in China. Despite the growth of online banking, a large number of Chinese consumers still do not trust online payment systems enough to complete their transactions there. This group of shoppers prefer to pay cash, or simply swipe their card in the deliverer's point of sales machine once the goods have reached them.

Digital Laws and Regulations in China

With the growth of e-commerce in the early 2000s and the increasing demands that came along with it, there have been important legal improvements. Yet, even today, the regulatory framework is rather fragmented, and sometimes, inconsistent, and therefore unevenly implemented. Regulations under the jurisdiction of MOFCOM (the Chinese Ministry of Commerce) and the MIIT (Ministry of Industry and Information Technology) are setting the rules for online commercial activities in China.

There is no explicit restriction or prohibition in Chinese commercial law with respect to setting up a commercial website through a third-party platform. In reality, the feasibility of establishing e-commerce activities depends on the requirements set by the third-party service providers. Tmall, for instance, requires that the sellers have a registered company in China. If you opt for a standalone website outside China, you will be operating from a server located abroad, and because your services will not be provided within the Chinese territory, your company will, of course, not be subject to the ICP (Internet content provider) requirements. There is always the risk that your site could be blocked by the Chinese authorities at any time without notice. In the event that content contravening Chinese laws and policies appears on your website, it can be blocked immediately. If your company has a commercial or non-commercial ICP license, you should normally be given the chance to remove the contravening content.

The conditions under which foreign investors can establish and operate a standalone e-commerce website have been the subject of much debate. Although the local government opened e-commerce to wholly foreign-owned investment in 2004, it was not clear whether e-commerce was included under retail, and as a consequence, e-commerce activities remained restricted for quite a long time. It was only in 2010 when

MOFCOM issued a notice to clarify the situation indicating that FIEs (foreign-invested enterprises) holding a trading or production license could directly engage in e-commerce activities without having to go through any additional approval process. It should be noted that the application of the MOFCOM notice has only been enforced by a number local authorities. Therefore, foreign companies with production or trading licenses seeking to engage in Chinese e-commerce should approach their provincial and local authorities to specify the applicable requirements.

The ICP license is also a subject of much debate. All laws under the jurisdiction of the MOFCOM function as regulators of China's information and communications industry. According to these laws, a commercial ICP license is required for a company to be able to provide commercial Internet information services. Yet, when a company sells its own products through the Internet, it is not considered a commercial Internet information activity. In this case, a non-commercial ICP license would be enough, and it is much easier to obtain. It is only in the case when a company offers its online platform to other companies that a commercial ICP license would be required. The trading of physical goods has been exempted from the commercial ICP license. Applying for a commercial ICP license is a very time-consuming procedure for foreign companies. According to my experience, Chinese authorities are rather unwilling to issue these licenses to foreign companies.

It is well-known that in China, all Internet traffic coming from foreign servers is directed through gateways controlled by the Chinese authorities. Sensitive content can be blocked or censored before reaching the general population. The Chinese online business environment is heavily regulated. Foreign companies are also indirectly affected by regulations on tax, import, foreign exchange, and online payments. Regulations are a complicated matter and will not be discussed in detail in this volume. Nonetheless, it is important for foreign companies to be aware that, if their server is not registered in China and if their website operates from their home country, service is likely to be affected because this redirection will cause operations to slow down. The table on the next page provides a list of relevant legislation that you can use as an initial reference in your search of the legal requirements applying to your particular industry and product category.

Relevant legislation	
Regulations on FIEs: MOFCOM and NDRC	• Catalog for the guidance of foreign investment industries • Provisions for the administration of foreign investment industries • Notice on issues related to examination, approval, and administration of online sales projects of FIEs
Regulations on telecommunications enterprises: MIIT	• Measures for the administration of Internet information services • Provisions on the administration of telecommunications enterprises with foreign investment
Other regulations	• Administrative measures on Internet information services • Provisions on the administration of foreign-invested telecom enterprises • Telecommunications regulations of the People's Republic of China • Interim measures for the administration of online commodities trading • Measures for the administration of telecom service operations

The Chinese government has been quite supportive toward the development of the e-commerce industry. Over the recent years, a set of guiding opinions and key rules has been promulgated as part of the effort to better regulate e-commerce. For example, in mid-2013, the measure for the management of public invoices was issued by the State Administration for Taxation. According to this measure, online retail platforms need to issue official invoices with each online purchase. This is part of the government's efforts to better regulate the Chinese online retail market. These measures are not expected to have a massive impact on purchases directly from major B2C platforms, as many are already providing their customers with such invoices. However, it might cause prices to increase on C2C websites like Taobao where many individual merchants who previously did not issue official invoices are now forced by law to do so.

Key Strategies for Different Company Types

While many Chinese companies have come to realize that the Internet is a great sales tool and already use it or are planning to use it as such, multinational companies have been rather slow to enter this fast-growing channel. This leaves a great deal of space for entrepreneurs and SMEs to enter the Chinese e-commerce market without having to face the amount of competition they would if they chose to make this move five years from now. All the individuals and companies that do recognize these opportunities must understand that entering the Chinese e-merging market will require a customized strategy. Most Chinese consumers, particularly the middle class living in urban centers, have shown their preference for multichannel shopping. In the next couple of years, multichannel shoppers will account for nearly half of the country's urban consumers. Considering this, it would not be a smart strategy for companies to focus solely on an offline or an online strategy.

Another factor is that consumer needs vary. As we have already discussed, heavy spenders have different shopping habits and needs from their light-spending counterparts. Consumers across different parts of China are looking for different products. You have to be clear right from the start about who your target customers are, where they live, and what their specific needs and wants are. Different types of companies will face different challenges, and hence will need to adapt their strategies according to the particularities of their respective customer segments.

Strategies for E-tailers

Strategies for e-tailers have been extensively discussed. Whether they are established or start-up companies, e-tailers face a big growth potential as the online commerce market is going to quadruple in the next years. They have a window of opportunity at their disposal, which they can use to establish their brand image and win customer loyalty before retailers develop their own online capabilities. E-tailers need to determine right from the start which customers they want to target and which product categories they want to participate in. Once they have done that, they will need to build innovative business models and address unmet needs of specific customer groups. To succeed in this step, they will need to meet some conditions:

> *Create unique product offerings.* For example, by venturing into new or growing product categories where Taobao has not yet established a dominant position. One such category is high-end fashion.
>
> *Build a targeted service.* It is crucial for e-tailers to think how they can offer different and customized services to their target segments, not only to the increasingly large numbers of light and heavy spenders, but also to the myriads of those new consumers from third- and fourth-tier regions who join the ranks of Chinese e-shoppers every year.
>
> *Offer compelling value propositions.* E-tailers must offer distinct value propositions such as a more customized service or product and a more appealing interface to differentiate themselves from competitors. Additionally, e-tailers will face the challenge of distinguishing themselves in terms of logistics capabilities, from warehouse and facilities set up to after-sales service.

Strategies for Retailers

E-commerce is a great opportunity for retailers to increase their footprint in China, an otherwise costly task. Like most companies, retailers need to first decide which role e-commerce will play within their overall corporate strategy. If they wait too long before deciding on their China strategy, they will risk losing their online relevance to companies that are exclusively web-based. Unlike the traditional patterns in developed markets where brick-and-mortar usually comes first, in China, companies have the possibility to grow online and offline at the same time. Rather than seeing online and offline as two independent strategies or as two stand-alone businesses, it is essential to treat them as integral parts of a single business model and to develop long-lasting relationships with the most profitable and dedicated multichannel customers.

This can be achieved with the following guidelines:

Drive traffic from physical stores to online storefronts and vice versa. Brick-and-mortar retailers especially need to think about how they can use their existing stores to their best advantage. It is actually the ability to direct customers in physical stores to their online platforms that gives retailers a competitive edge over e-tailers. Building their brand image will help them boost consumer traffic well beyond the confines of their physical store. It is common for Chinese consumers to decide on a brand and a specific product online and ultimately complete the purchase online. This applies in cases of high reliability and good after-sales service, which are essential with products such as consumer electronics.

Target consumers through the right offerings and pricing. Because 20 percent of online purchases are products that consumers cannot find offline, companies that build credibility and trust in terms of offerings and pricing, will be able to provide a larger selection of products online than in their physical stores.

Decide on a service and logistics solution. Store-based logistics usually limit distribution. Additional investment will be required for the company to be able to manage orders and delivery for customers who are based far from the company's physical network. In this case, it is advisable to either use a third-party logistics provider or build your own delivery network if large volumes and special handling are needed.

Online mindset. It is essential for retailers to learn to think and act like e-tailers. If they keep a brick-and-mortar perspective and view their online presence as an add-on only, they risk underestimating the potential rewards.

Strategies for Brand Companies

The need for action is particularly critical for brand companies competing in the fastest-growing categories: consumer electronics, travel, casual wear, and cosmetics. First, they need to decide what kind of online presence they want to have and what role e-commerce should play in their brand strategy. To determine this, they will need to understand their target customers' online and offline shopping habits, as well as their default shopping destinations. Identifying which of their online needs remain unmet is also essential. There is a variety of possible approaches companies can use to identify target customers and determine the best way to reach them online. Again, this strategy will be determined by the specifics of the industry your products fall into and by the geographic areas you want to target.

Brand companies need to be very clear about their unique selling points and focus their efforts on developing a strong brand image to attract consumers. Important efforts should be directed toward targeting customer segments that are not yet served by the brand's main retail channels. It is also crucial for brand companies to weight the implications that an e-commerce strategy will have on their offline agenda. If fulfillment is satisfactory through e-commerce, it might be a good move to scale back a part of your offline presence. For example, stocking enough products in your retail stores to encourage first-time trial purchases while dedicating your e-tail channel to repeat purchases. To complement your offline presence, a solid integration of both online and offline strategies is required.

In crafting their e-commerce strategy, brand companies have various options to choose from. They all come with tradeoffs, of course: an independent and dedicated brand website allows the company full control of the brand image and lets them define the consumer experience. The downside is that it will be hard and costly to drive significant traffic to a standalone website. For many companies, Taobao and Tmall remain the best way to attract a large amount of traffic without having to invest in online advertising and marketing, but it will be difficult for these brand companies to offer a consumer experience distinct from that offered by competitor companies also selling on these platforms.

After deciding on the format, companies need to plan their go-to market strategy from the range of products they will sell online to the management of accomplishing sales. You should consider the following questions: Should you offer the same SKUs (stock-keeping units) offline as online? Would you rather limit the choices or even decide to make some products exclusively available online? Should you use distributor channels to open stores, which translates into greater reach, but also loss of control? Or, should you rather manage directly your own stores and delivery service? It is equally important that brand companies plan carefully their margin structure by taking into account both offline and online trade economics.

Brand companies that choose to focus solely on online strategies will face a difficult incentives challenge. For instance, the advantages inherent in not having to pay operational costs and rent could make it possible to lower the prices of products sold online. Nonetheless, such discounts can potentially create conflicts with the distributors or franchisees that sell your products at full price. To avoid these issues, it is necessary to design a cross-channel conflicts plan well in advance.

The Multichannel Advantage

A sure bet for any type of company is to address the growing trend among consumers toward multichannel online shopping. Most consumers visit several websites for different product categories, and their need for multiple options is growing. Consumers who use more than one channel to shop are three to five times more profitable than e-shoppers who follow a single channel. It is, therefore, crucial for companies to carefully manage their online presence and attract customers using a variety of online options.

Do have in mind that offering an online experience only will not be sufficient. The offline, physical experience is bound to remain a major factor influencing consumers' purchase decisions. More than 50 percent of Chinese consumers pay visits to offline retail stores before proceeding to an online purchase. Other consumers search online first and then visit the store to get a better idea of the look and feel of the product they intend to buy, while others start with the intention of buying from the store, but they reach the final decision on what to buy online afterward. An offline presence is not necessary for a company to be successful in the Chinese e-commerce market. Yet, given the rising demand for improved service and quality, it could provide the basis for better customer service and further differentiation from online-only companies. This is particularly relevant in product categories where customers need to exchange the goods (e.g., in the case of apparel) or repair them (as in the case of consumer electronics).

Online-only companies should seriously think of ways to build an integrated offline strategy. For offline companies, a multichannel strategy will leverage offline assets and increase brand trust, thus exposing their products or services to larger crowds of e-shoppers.

Managing Practical Challenges

Customs

One of the major issues that companies often face when doing business in or with China is the issue of taxes and duties imposed on merchandise imported into China. Companies shipping their products to China will have to be prepared to pay customs tariffs depending on the value and volume of the goods. B2C shipments do not belong to the category of personal effects and *theoretically* (I hope you are getting the meaning of my use of italics!) cannot be cleared as such. They should normally go through the general customs clearance process, in which case, the importer or receiver of the products needs to register at the local customs authority. Customs tariffs are likely to discourage Chinese consumers from purchasing goods directly from foreign e-commerce websites based outside of China. Although there are variations in rates and regulations from product to product, there are general tax norms to be followed by merchants.

There are three types of taxes your company will most probably go through when importing products into China: VAT (value-added tax), consumption tax, and customs duties.

VAT for Imported Goods

All goods imported to China are subject to a VAT. The applicable tax rates are the same as the ones applied to goods sold in the domestic market (typically 13–17 percent for most product categories). VAT is generally payable on the customs clearance day.

Consumption Tax for Imported Goods

Imported goods subject to consumption tax include luxury products such as high-energy consumption goods, high-end watches, and non-renewable petroleum goods. Import consumption tax is normally calculated on a value or quantity basis with considerable variations in tax amounts and rates. It should be paid within two weeks counting from the day that the consumption tax bill of payment is issued.

Customs Duties

This category includes both import and export duties with a total of more than 8,200 taxed items. Customs duties are calculated based on product value or product quantity. Import duties depend on a number of variables.

General Duty Rates

General duty rates are normally applied to imports originating from countries or territories that are not included in any agreements or treaties with China, or imports from unknown places of origin.

Conventional Duty Rates

This type of rate is applied to imports originating from countries that have signed regional trade agreements with China, including the following agreements:

- The Asia-Pacific Trade Agreement conventional duty rates which are applied to 1,875 imports from South Korea, India, Sri Lanka, Bangladesh, and Laos.
- Products imported from ASEAN (Association of Southeast Asian Nations) member countries.
- Chile, Pakistan, New Zealand, Singapore, Peru, and Costa Rica are subject to conventional duty rates under the relevant free trade agreements. Some imports from Hong Kong, Macau, and Taiwan enjoy tariff-free policies.

MFN Tax Rates

Most-favored-nation (MFN) tax rates are the most common duties applied to imports. They are generally much lower than the tax rates imposed to non MFN countries. They apply to the following categories of goods:

- Imports from WTO (World Trade Organization) member countries
- Imports from countries or territories that have signed bilateral agreements with China
- Imports originated from China

Special Preferential Tax Rates

Special preferential tax rates are typically applied to imports originating from countries or territories included in trade agreements, which contain special preferential tax provisions with China. The rates are generally lower than MFN rates and conventional duty rates.

Under the 2013 Tariff Plan, special preferential duty rates are applied to certain goods originating from the 40 least developed countries as classified by the United Nations. These countries include Ethiopia, Rwanda, and Afghanistan.

Tariff Rate Quota Tax Rates

Under tariff rate quota (TRQ) schemes, lowered tariff rates are applied to products imported within the quota. For example, according to the 2013 Tariff Plan, the TRQ rate for importing wheat within the quota is 1 percent, substantially lower than the MFN duty rate of 65 percent and the general duty rate of 80 percent.

Temporary Duty Rates

China occasionally imposes temporary tax rates to a number of imported goods. To boost imports and meet domestic demand in 2013, China implemented temporary tax rates lower than the MFN tariff on more than 780 imported commodities, including seasoning products, pacemakers, special-formula infant milk powder, and resources, including kaolin, alfalfa, and eiderdown.

Other Tax Rates

Considerably higher rates are generally implemented to goods originating from countries or regions that violate trade agreements with
China: Chinese regulations regarding anti-dumping, anti-subsidies, and
safeguard measures. Retaliatory tariffs could also be applied.

Logistics

So far, Chinese e-commerce has benefited from low shipping fees, but
otherwise, it has been significantly impeded by an inadequate logistics
infrastructure. Most e-sellers are obliged to rely heavily on local small
delivery companies. It is, in fact, the e-commerce industry that is the
major driving force behind the growth of the parcel delivery infrastructure in China. It is estimated that 75 percent of revenues from package deliveries in 2017 came from e-commerce activities. Taobao alone
accounted for more than half of all domestic deliveries.

As the logistics infrastructure is still in its nascent stages of development in China, it is not uncommon to experience late deliveries,
damaged or lost goods, unprofessional attitudes from delivery staff, and
disappointing return procedures. A lack of capabilities is one of the major
issues impeding the development of the Chinese e-commerce industry.
Given the inefficiency of the infrastructure, delivery concerns are cited
among the top reasons that make consumers feel hesitant to buy products
online. Very often, their major concern is not a high shipping cost or the
risk of their goods getting damaged or lost during delivery, but the worry
that their goods will be substituted with fakes. For these reasons, many
online consumers often choose e-tailers whose distribution centers are
based in their city.

Most Chinese e-commerce companies usually hire third-party express
delivery service providers. Merchants selling through Tmall are required
to choose one of those express delivery companies. Providers such as
Shunfeng, Shentong, or Yuantong offer basic delivery services and do not
provide services such as COD, exchanges, or returns. International companies like FedEx, UPS, TNT, and DHL cover smaller areas, but have a
reputation for providing more reliable and consistent delivery services.

Other services these companies offer include COD, customized delivery, and warehousing.

I always recommend foreign companies to use regional service providers if they want to target specific cities. In the event they need to ship inland or to remote provinces, they should consider companies such as EMS or providers covering larger areas. The latter tend to be most costly though. If your company deals with large volumes of goods or if your goods need special handling, a good idea might be to consider setting up your own distribution network.

The Future of E-Commerce and Technology in China

China has done quite a journey to get where it is today. When the economic reforms of the late 1970s began, the world saw China as a developing nation trying hard to catch up with the pace of the West. Then, manufacturing centers began to pop up in Southern China, and people saw it as a toy factory. After that, it was seen as the copying and pirating capital of the world. Many did not believe that a—so-called—Communist country could transition to a wider market economy integrated with the rest of the world or move beyond the manufacturing chain by producing high-quality, cutting-edge technology products. Although changes are taking place, such as rising labor costs and other countries expanding their manufacturing sectors, China will not lose its place as the world's factory. With the growth in manufacturing came a wealth of technology transfer and a great deal of tech-related products. Now China is accomplishing what many thought was impossible. It is moving swiftly into the age of innovation and well ahead of the rest of the world in some areas.

Most of the world's smartphones and computers are made in Chinese factories. Most of those factories are located in and around the Pearl River Delta. Device components are largely made in China and assembled there as well. A combination of key resources, manufacturing infrastructure, powerful tech companies, incubators, supply chains, and international transport. The region is also known as *Silicon Delta*. This region is emerging from a phase that experienced ideas, visions, and designs developed abroad with product and hardware execution done locally. Now, both are happening in the same place and at record speeds, thus attracting international and local talent. Many established Chinese brands are also making their mark on a global level. Lenovo is a case in point. The company is second globally when it comes to PC sales, right behind Hewlett Packard, while Huawei's 2017 global smartphone sales exceeded Apple's, placing it in second place, behind Korean Samsung. And, this goes far beyond manufacturing and sales.

Homegrown tech companies now compete on a global scale in terms of innovation, service quality, brand recognition, and partnerships. Alibaba is a good example. It entered the scene as a long-term Olympic Sponsor in 2018, just as McDonalds exited. It provided cloud services, digital media, and e-commerce platforms for the winter Olympics that took place in Pyeongchang and assisted the International Olympic Committee (IOC) to find ways to save money on future games. Also, Alibaba's first global ad campaign focuses on values such as sportsmanship, underdogs, and generosity. These developments are no accident. Local and national authorities are involved. Beijing is the leading tech hub in the world, followed by Berlin and San Francisco. The central government is supporting cities like Chengdu and Guiyang, as they develop their own tech hubs. While China still remains behind in some areas, 2018 was a benchmark year for many of the country's national brands. China's evolution is evident and unstoppable.

How does this evolution translate in terms of facts and figures and real-world examples in 2018?

Supercomputing

China currently owns 202 of the world's 500 most powerful and fast supercomputers—including the top two—compared with the United States' 143. The top American computer ranked fifth behind China, Switzerland, and Japan. In 2018, China had the fastest supercomputers in the world for the 9th year in a row. Since 2016, Chinese high-tech companies have been using only Chinese designed processors. China now intends to launch a new generation of exascale supercomputers. These are often described as *super supercomputers* and are capable of billion billion calculations per second.

Robotics

In 2015, the Chinese government devised the Robotics Industry Development Plan as part of an industry initiative called Made in China 2015. This five-year plan aims to expand the robotics sector. China aims to manufacture at least 100,000 industrial robots per year by 2010. This is already being done with research and development, as well as through acquisition and investment. Midea Group, China's leading home appliance manufacturer, is an example in point. The company has recently acquired a majority stake in the German robot manufacturer Kuka GA, as well as Israeli motion solutions provider Servotronix Motion Control, so that it can integrate their technologies into its robotics.

China is also the world's largest and fastest-growing robotics market. It currently ranks number one in sales in terms of industrial robots, while South Korea and Japan are ranked second and third, respectively, with the United States ranking fourth. The global robotics market is currently worth about 30 billion U.S. dollars, and by 2019, China is expected to account for 40 percent of the global robotic sales, as opposed to 27 percent, back in 2015.

Virtual Reality

Virtual reality (VR) technology is currently very popular in China. Sales of VR headsets accounted for almost 60 percent of total VR product sales in China, while consumer content made up less than 8 percent. Consumer VR content sales are set to explode and are expected to account for 25.5 percent of VR revenues by 2021, with games leading this product category and generating 9.7 billion RMB, followed by movies at 8.8 billion RMB. China's state-owned broadcaster, CCTV, has bought VR technology from 7D Vision Tech—a Beijing-based production startup—to telecast events like basketball matches and the Spring Festival Gala. 7D Vision Tech has made half of their annual revenue from selling VR filming services to TCV stations.

Blockchain Technology

Blockchain technology was first officially mentioned in China in 2016 as part of the government's 13th Five-Year Plan. The government wants China to be a pioneer in this blockchain technology and wants to apply it to industry and commerce. Blockchain technology works like a set of digital fingerprints. This has made it ideal for online banking, digital contracts, secure tracking procedures, as well as peer-to-peer transactions.

This explains why many companies and governments globally are investing in this type of technology with a particular stress to applications that can increase security, speed, and services offered digitally. In China, however, it is widely accepted that blockchain technology will be applied in a highly controlled way, thus maintaining the current ban on bitcoin, ICOs, and other cryptocurrencies. The focus will be on improving the technology's security for potential use in finance. As of 2017, 550 blockchain technology-related patents were filed by Chinese companies, against 192 from South Korea and 284 from the United States. Many provincial governments are already proposing guidelines to attract companies that develop, design, and implement blockchain applications. Chengdu, Guangxi, and Hangzhou have proposed policies to encourage research and development in this field.

Drone Technology

DaJiang Innovations Ltd., a Shenzhen-based company, is currently the world leader in civilian drones. DaJiang have captured 70 percent of the market already. They enjoy an avid, large fan base. Their unmanned aerial vehicles (UAV) are used in aerial filming and photography. This technology has been used in productions like *Game of Thrones* and *American Ninja Warrior*. The company has even won an Emmy prize for its engineering creativity. Many major e-commerce players such as Alibaba, Jing Dong, and Tencent use drone delivery programs at advanced stages of development. The first official government license for drone deliveries was granted to SF Express, China's largest logistics firm in early 2018. This is going to impact remote areas of the country as it will allow rapid response in case of natural disasters and emergencies.

Financial Technology

Chinese financial technology (fintech) companies took the top three spots and five of the top 10 spots in the 2017 KPMG and H2 Ventures FinTech 100 list. The list ranks companies from around the world based on innovation, size, brand recognition, and capital-raising activity. This was the second year in a row for Ant Financial, an Alibaba affiliate, to top the list.

Artificial Intelligence

China is investing heavily in artificial intelligence (AI) technology, from algorithms to chips. The State Council has issued an ambitious policy for China to become the *primary artificial intelligence innovation center in the world* by 2030. Chinese startup Cambricon has designed a new chip that enables portable consumer devices to engage in the same level of AI that took 16,000 microprocessors to accomplish back in 2012. This would make them capable of navigating roads, recognizing faces, and translating languages. In the worldwide search for AI-enabled chips, Cambricon founders are leading the way, and their chip has already been recently used in a Huawei smartphone that they proudly call *the world's first real AI phone.* Cambricon was valued at one billion U.S. dollars in 2018.

Electric Cars

China is the largest car market in the world and the largest car producer. It is also the largest market for electric vehicles globally and the global leader in terms of electric vehicle production and investment. Chinese manufacturers do not sell the majority of the traditional vehicles they produce within China yet, but domestic companies have, nonetheless, a 90 percent market share in the electric vehicle arena.

Space Exploration

China is one of three nations—along with the United States and Russia—that can send both people and satellites into space. The China National Space Administration has sent numerous satellites into space and has partnered with European and Russian space agencies in various projects, including preparations for a manned mission to Mars. It has also set its sights on a moon landing by 2025 and is developing plans and capabilities for supersonic aircraft.

Green Energy Technology

China has been the world's largest manufacturer of solar panels since 2008. The country is also the leader in wind power generation.

It currently enjoys the largest wind power capacity in the world. China's 13th Five-Year Plan for Building Energy Efficiency and Green Building Development includes aggressive goals for renovation, green building construction, including a requirement for 50 percent of all new urban buildings to be certified *green buildings.*

Medical Big Data

Due to its large population and its efforts to improve its health-care system and its medical technology, China is the global center for medical data. It is the only place in the world where researchers can quickly pool information on 100,000 patients. In fact, the country is the world's largest genome database, which makes it a hub for genomic research and data. A growing number of startups specializing in health tech are engaged in partnerships in China to perfect algorithms, find new cures for diseases to be used in medical AI. China has also engaged in certain highly controversial research experiments. In 2015, Chinese researchers edited genes for the first time in an experiment during which they successfully removed puppy embryos from their mother, edited their genes to make them build muscle faster before reinserting them in their mother. In 2017, they successfully cloned dogs after having edited their genes.

Alibaba Group

Alibaba is the largest online retailer in the world. The company's gross merchandise volume reached 547 million U.S. dollars in 2017. Alibaba first started as an e-commerce business connecting sellers and buyers, taking advantage of China's growing Internet population and underdeveloped brick-and-mortar businesses. Founded in 1999 by Jack Ma, the company operates the largest online marketplaces in the world. Its ecosystem comprises digital media, e-commerce, logistics, cloud computing, digital marketing, and local services. Alibaba's mission is to make it easy to do business anywhere.

The Future of Chinese Retail

The New Retail Strategy was first introduced by Alibaba in 2016. At Alibaba's Computing Conference, Jack Ma's speech focuses on five main areas that are being transformed by technology and that are set to impact profoundly the industry in the foreseeable future. These areas include manufacturing, new energy, new finance, new technology with new retail at the center. New retail is Alibaba's strategy to redefine commerce by enabling seamless engagement between the online and offline worlds. The goal is not to convert online customers into offline customers. It goes far beyond. With new retail, Alibaba aims to use their technology capabilities to digitally transform offline retail in China, which currently accounts for 82 percent of the total retail volume. New retail is about building a retail ecosystem that blends online and offline channels in a unified way, featuring the consumer at the center.

The concept of a uni-channel plays a key role in this strategy. The term used to refer to companies that offered products only through one outlet, usually a standard, physical store with limited advertising options (mainly radio, local press, and so on). Recently, the meaning of this term has changed to catch up with the rapid market changes that are taking place. Multi- and uni-channel marketing are now making use of both online and offline marketing opportunities. The ultimate goal is to be ever-present. Many brands give their customers inconsistent experiences across the different channels they use. The aim is to place the customer at the center of these interactions and create a uniform experience. Therefore, a uni-channel strategy, as Alibaba defines it, refers to a unified channel with the customer at its center, offering a global, tailored shopping experience. This strategy blurs the line between online and offline, thus redefining the role of a brand's online presence.

This enables merchants to stay relevant in China's dynamic digital economy landscape and offers brand-building and sales growth opportunities. New retail is about to transform every aspect of the retail value chain, from merchandising to logistics, without the need for expertise and in-depth tech knowledge. To showcase their vision, Alibaba used the 2017 Singles' Day Festival as a way to transform retail, by being 18 times bigger than Amazon Prime Day and three times bigger than Black Friday and Cyber Monday combined.

Retail sales are a lynchpin in China's national strategy for economic growth. Many believe this will rewrite the future of retail in China and beyond. It is not only Alibaba that shapes the commercial landscape in China though. Other companies, like Tencent and JD, are supporting this strategy. This is leading to rapid change, as well as growing competition. The core rivalry in China's digital space is between Alibaba and Tencent. Retail and payment systems are at the heart of their rivalry.

Based on these trends, this is what the future of e-tail in China looks like:

Smart Stores

In the era of smartphones and digital shopping, the emergence of *smart stores* is no surprise. The major features of smart stores include:

- A connection to an online payment system is required for customers to be able to enter the store.
- Facial recognition technology is used to track customers. Discounts are offered on items they smile at or on items that they have searched online.
- Customer's purchasing behavior data, facial recognition information, memberships, and customer service history are all stored and tracked.
- Price tags are electronic and prices vary in real time based on certain factors.
- Home delivery details do not need to be provided by the customer, as the system has already on record their address information.
- Delivery in major Chinese cities takes from 15 minutes to three hours maximum.

- Customers can try on apparel and make up products virtually, using what Alibaba calls a *magic mirror*. With the help of radiofrequency identification and augmented reality technology, items are displayed on an accurately measured avatar of you. This technology can also be used to see what a piece of furniture looks like in one's home or to tour overseas properties.
- Innovative technologies, such as the Cloud Shelf, a screen that replaces shelves in a store, use radiofrequency identification technology to identify product tags, display the item's availability, color and size options, and customer reviews. The customer can buy the item by simply scanning its QR code.

Many of these features are already being integrated to non-commercial spaces such as smart nursing rooms that are connected online so that parents can find them more easily. These rooms are equipped with screens that can be used to look for childcare items such as diapers, which can be purchased while mothers use the room. The aim of these innovations and data collection is to personalize the shopping experience. Each customer's experience from advertising to pricing will be determined by data on an individual level, and no two people will experience the same journey. All aspects of the consumer experience will be intertwined and operate in concert for the ultimate convenience and excitement of the consumer.

Blurring of the Line Between Consumer and Advertiser

This is already taking place in China, as many companies reward customers for posting their purchases on social media, but it is going to happen in a more sophisticated and embedded fashion offline in the future. For instance, one of the brands that were part of the 2017 Singles' Day Festival, after a customer bought an item, a photo studio in the store had staff to quickly put on professional make up and take their picture with the item using sophisticated lighting in a studio settings. The resulting photo was stylish, ad quality, and campaign-ready. Hence, the consumer now becomes a mini-influencer and an active partner in social selling. In late 2017, Tencent officially announced its *Smart +* strategy using its cloud platform establishing a smart ecosystem covering retail, marketing, logistics, finance, communication, and more. Tencent also aims to execute Smart + Retail with the latest Big Data, AI technology, and cloud computing. Meanwhile, existing WeChat features, such as mini programs, official accounts, and WeChat Pay, already support retail sellers and brands. Big Data analysis and WeChat Pay allow merchants to better understand their target consumers and customize messages and promotions quite precisely. With mini programs, merchants can merge shopping experiences and output services of both online and offline retail in a smooth manner.

Retail as Entertainment

Modern Chinese consumers are predominantly young and mobile-savvy, so shopping is not just about passively adding items to their virtual shopping art. Shopping has evolved into a social activity, a means of consuming content, and ultimately, a form of entertainment. For example, cloth shopping can be done virtually in the—virtual—company of one's friends. Clothes can be chosen specifically for users, based on their data and shopping history. Users can try them on virtually, compare items with their friends, and get their opinions about the clothes. Then, they can purchase the items they like and have them delivered so that they arrive at their address before they return home that day. After that, pictures of the customers wearing the new items can be sent to the brand to enter a contest and later be used in advertising campaigns.

Tmall Neighborhood Convenience Stores

Alibaba is developing new retail models that are transforming many retail experiences from the local grocery store, the shopping mall, and the car dealership. The company is working closely with merchants and brands to incubate the available technology, so that it can be leveraged by the whole retail industry. Alibaba's LST system is different from Amazon's physical store push, in that it can be leveraged for use by millions of local convenience stores to digitize their businesses, rather than only be used in Alibaba-owned stores. For instance, this system can help the owner of a physical retail store to measure the demographics and purchasing behaviors of surrounding customers, then predict and recommend the most in-demand products for sales in that store. Their technology capabilities can be leveraged for logistics, merchandising, as well as inventory management to enhance their business operations.

Major *See Now, Buy Now* online fashion shows have already taken place in 2016 and 2017 and organized by brands like Pandora, Guerlain, MAC, and so on. During these shows, customers are invited to do more than just watch. They can buy their preferred outfits using a purchase link that is displayed on the left side of the screen on Taobao or Tmall. Alternatively, viewers can shake their phones to go to the product page, in case they are watching the show on TV.

Gamification

Alibaba launched a gaming campaign called *Catch the Cat* in 2016, after witnessing the popularity of location-based, augmented reality game Pokemon Go. The cat people were trying to catch was Tmall's mascot. In 2017, 65 established brands like P&G, MAC, Pizza Hut, Disneyworld, and KFC participated in this gaming campaign that encourages Chinese consumers to visit their retail stores. Alibaba continued the *Catch the Cat* in 2017. Users were invited to access the game interface on the Taobao or Tmall application on their smartphone to catch 170 different types of virtual cats that appeared randomly. Each cat was related to a designated brand. Once caught, users could get a game card with a special discount or prize that they could use when they made purchases in the brand's Tmall store. Tmall's cat mascot was also featured in thousands of brand stores across China, such as Starbucks, where users could catch these virtual cats.

China's 2020 Social Ranking System

It seems that Big Brother is coming to town! China is about to develop its social credit system, a system that is highly integrated with Big Data and technology. In mid-2017, the Chinese government began generating an 18-digit personal identification number for everyone in the country. This number is associated with what is essentially an economic and reputational identity card. Credit scores are no new. They were introduced about 70 years ago in the United States, while FICO scores are still used to determine a person's loan eligibility. China did not use similar ratings and credit systems until very recently and very few people in the country had access to them. In the search for a system to fill this void, authorities have opted for a system that takes into account more criteria. This new score takes into account a wide variety of offline and online behavior and amounts to a background check, credit score, Internet activity history, Google deep dive, reference check, and family interview, all in one. The government's stated goal is to enhance safety and trust, especially in regard to food production and to help enforce integrity in business.

By 2020 all Chinese citizens will be enrolled in this vast national database. This will apply to both individuals and businesses. So far, it is not clear whether foreign companies operating in China will be subject to this rating system or not.

Information will be stored on the country's unified credit information platform and will collect financial information (bank account, loan and mortgage data), business registration information, tax reports, social security payment statistics, traffic violation statistics, commercial activities, social behavior, lawful and unlawful behavior, as well as online activities. The program has already been implemented in 12 Chinese cities. The database has collected information from 44 government departments, including provinces and cities, as well as from 60 private organizations. Two companies were licensed to assist in the development of this system: Ant Financial's Sesame Credit and China Rapid Finance. The former rates users based partly on their purchases through Alipay, while the latter is an online consumer-lending platform and Tencent partner. Sesame Credit has also worked with Didi Chuxing, a taxi hailing service, and Baihe, China's largest online matchmaking service. So, it has access to a very wide selection of data.

The question is how this rating system is going to impact people's everyday lives? For those with high social credit scores, rewards may range from pre-approved loans of RMB 5,000 to RMB 50,000, to deposit-less car rentals, faster hotel check-ins, or fast-tracked applications for EU Schengen visas. High scores are about to become a status symbol is some circles, with some users boasting about their high scores online.

What happens then to those with lower or low scores? Low scores may, in fact, result in slower Internet speeds, restricted access to restaurants, private schools, golf courses, the removal of one's right to travel freely abroad. It can even lead to restricted access to social security benefits. Certain jobs in law, civil service, or journalism may be off limits. The principle is that, if trust is broken in one place, restrictions will be imposed everywhere.

People have, naturally, raised concerns about this and require that the system takes certain circumstances into consideration, so that, if, for instance, a person misses or delays a bill payment because they are ill in the hospital, it will not affect their general score and punishments will not ensue. The close collaboration between the Chinese government and digital giants for social data provision initially raised concerns about consumer privacy. Many fear that a close monitoring of their daily activities on social media platforms and e-commerce sites, such as purchasing a product or posting a comment, will restrict their freedom of digital expression. This rating system takes on a new dimension when considered along with the fact that China has the world's largest genome database: the China National GeneBank, which has more than 500 million genetic sequences and the computational power and AI to deal with them.

Many feel, however, that the establishment of a more complete credit system will be ultimately beneficial to Chinese citizens, especially in terms of financial security. By leveraging the advantages of China's most successful tech companies, China will be able to reinforce profitable behavior, improve its social mechanisms, and better integrate with emerging global trends.

China Going Global

China has gone from a place shut off from the world to a manufacturing center, to a place that Western companies coveted for its huge consumer base. Then, China developed its own companies that were outside the state-owned system. These companies succeeded within China, and now, contrary to the predictions of many, are succeeding and becoming known globally. Additionally, Chinese business interests are acquiring foreign companies, taking on global assets.

Chinese Brands Known Globally

Aside from the companies that have been discussed in detail, such as Alibaba, WeChat, and others, here are some examples of local Chinese brands, largely unknown outside of the country 10 years ago, that are now players on the global stage.

Lenovo

The company is currently the largest PC manufacturer in the world, the biggest seller of smartphones in China, and a globally known brand since 2005. Once a small company known for its cheap ThinkPad computers, it has acquired and merged with other technology companies and is now a conglomerate with headquarters in both Beijing and North Carolina, United States. Lenovo started to become an international brand name when it acquired IBM's PC division in 2005. Its acquisitions include Motorola Mobility, as well as Brazilian and German tech companies. Most of these acquisitions were made to help the company gain access to international markets.

Huawei

A multinational telecommunications company with its headquarters in Shenzhen, China, Huawei is the largest telecommunications manufacturer in the world. The company is a global leader in 5G technology. It designs its own chips, supplies equipment for and builds telecommunications infrastructure globally. This includes cloud services, Internet service equipment, as well as traditional phone technology. Most of the world's largest providers—including Vodafone, British Telecom, T-Mobile, Bell Canda, and Portugal Telecom—have worked with Huawei at some point. The company also has a successful smartphone division that plans to launch one of the world's first 5G handsets while it has announced plans to launch a blockchain-enabled phone.

Haier

Haier is a multinational consumer electronics and appliance company headquartered in Quingdao, Shandong Province. The company was a pioneer in the country's globalization drive and was one of the first Chinese companies to successfully expand into international markets. It has been the largest home appliance company in the world for eight years in a row, with 12 percent of market share in 2017. The brand is also known for developing business strategies that differ from those of other large corporations and is constantly updating their approaches. Haier recently bought General Electric Appliances and is focusing on its e-commerce presence and Internet-related products.

Hisense

Hisense is similar to Haier, in that it is also a large, Qingdao-based electronics manufacturer. It is a state-owned company that has some publicly traded subsidiaries. The brand might be lesser known in terms of its major product lines because they sell their products under a variety of brand names that they have acquired through brand licensing deals, company acquisitions, and partnerships. Hisense has acquired product lines and selling rights to products from Toshiba, Sharp, Hitachi, NEC, Qualcomm, and Sanyo. The brand is better known for their smartphones, smart TVs, as well as its high-profile sports-related promotional activities such as the naming rights to the Hisense Arena in Melbourne, its partnership with FIFA, and its sponsorship of the 2016 Euro football championships.

Xiaomi

The company became known as a mobile phone manufacturer and was a key player in the Chinese market as smartphones were becoming more popular. Xiaomi is the fifth best-selling smartphone manufacturer in China, right behind Apple. It is the second largest in India and ranks in the top 10 worldwide. Although the company suffered some setbacks in recent years, it has staged a comeback and is now a globally known brand in the smartphone sector.

Anker

Anker is a Changsha-based Chinese company founded in 2011. They have offices in Shenzhen and Seattle. They are one of the world's most popular brands for portable power banks. Anker was one of the first brands to master this product category by selling on Amazon. It still channels its sales and delivery operations there to serve their Western customers. Within China, the company sells on Tmall and JD.com. Their products regularly feature in top 10 lists of the best rechargers. The company is now branching out into new product areas such as portable projectors and equipment for smart homes.

DJI

DJI stands for DaJiang Innovation. The company was founded in 2006 by Frank Wang, a student at the Hong Kong University of Science and Technology, which offered him a grant to study and develop drone technology. Headquartered in Shenzhen, the company is renowned for its unmanned flying machines that are optimized for filming and photo purposes. The company has won a technology Emmy, and they enjoy a 66 percent share of the North American market for drones in the 1,000 to 2,000 U.S. dollars price range and a 68 percent share in the 2,000–4,000 U.S. dollars range.

OnePlus

Founded in 2013, OnePlus is the youngest company on this list. One of its founders is the former vice president of Oppo, a big smartphone brand in China. Oppo is the primary and only institutional investor of OnePlus. Its first phone was called One Plus One, which is abbreviated as OPO. The brand made its mark by selling initially only through pre-sale and only on the Internet. This led to the development of a growing number of dedicated followers. Its smartphones were flagship quality, but at a much lower price. The company still operates this way, with the exception of invitations and pre-sales. Its smartphones have evolved and are among the most advanced phones in the market.

Global Brands Now Owned by Chinese Companies

The brands listed here were founded and came to prominence in Western markets. They are strongly connected with certain countries, nationalities, philosophies, and lifestyles. It might come as a surprise to some readers that they are now owned by Chinese companies.

- **IBM**: Owned by Lenovo
- **Motorola:** Owned by Lenovo
- **General Electric Appliances**: Owned by Haier
- **Volvo Cars**: Owned by Zhejiang Geely Holding Group
- **Club Med:** Majority owned by Fosun International Ltd.
- **London Black Cabs:** Owned by Zhejiang Geely Holding Group
- **Pizza Express:** Owned by Chinese Private Equity firm Hony Capital
- **Harvey Nichols**: Owned by Dickson Concepts
- **Inter Milan:** Owned by Suning Holdings Group
- **AC Milan:** Majority owned by Chinese Company Rossoneri Sport Investment Co.
- **Aston Villa:** Majority owned by Chinese company Recon Sports Ltd.
- **The Ironman Triathlon:** Organizer Triathlon Corporation is owned by Wanda Group
- **Grindr:** Owned by game developer Beijing Kunlun Tech
- **The Wardorf Astoria**: Owned by Anbang Insurance Group

- **Corbis Image Licensing**: Founded by Bill Gates, now owned by Unity Glory International, a subsidiary of the Visual China Group, the exclusive distributor of Getty images in China
- **500 px**: Popular photo site similar to Flickr, now owned by Visual China Group
- **AMC Theaters**: Owned by Chinese conglomerate Wanda Group. This acquisition made Wanda Group the owner of the largest theater chain in the world
- **Legendary Entertainment**, producer of films like Batman, Godzilla, Inception, The Dark Knight: Owned by Wanda Group

Final Thoughts and Recommendations

E-commerce in China is here to stay. The Chinese online consumer population is huge and will keep steadily growing for the next 10 years. Starting from a low base 14 years ago, Chinese e-shoppers are nowadays more and more eager to buy any sort of products online, from electronics and clothes to books and food. Platform websites, and especially Taobao, have played a major role in boosting online consumption, while payment mechanisms such as Alipay have contributed to making consumers more confident when completing their online purchases. For foreign entrepreneurs and SMEs, e-commerce is a great way to access the Chinese market without having to invest directly. Marketplaces offer a relatively low-cost way of promoting your goods to an existing large audience while avoiding the hassle of ICP licensing. However, simply setting up a Tmall storefront or building a standalone website will not bring the desired results unless your strategy is combined with the right marketing and CRM management tools.

We have discussed how enormous the potential of the Chinese e-commerce industry is. Realizing this potential will also depend on improvements made in the country's productivity and infrastructure. Other emerging economies can draw on China's e-commerce success to foster entrepreneurship. For these economies, early-stage priorities should be to develop the necessary technology infrastructure. Before embarking in any e-commerce activity in China, the whole process should be considered very carefully step by step: from when customers click on *buy* to when the goods are delivered to their door. After-sales service should also be taken seriously. With respect to the logistics strategy your company will decide to follow, it is important to target the cities first, and carefully choose the right logistics providers that you will use to deliver your products.

Whether you choose a third-party platform or your own website, be aware that great marketing efforts need to be deployed to make your product stand out among the multitude of other online offerings.

Make good use of all available online marketing tools, including SEO, keyword research, and Chinese social media platforms. With regard to third-party platforms, make sure you understand how the ranking systems work. Losing half a star from your Taobao ranking is likely to have a significant impact on the sales. Do not underestimate the time, financial, and human resources required to build and maintain your online offering. Marketplace websites need to be monitored constantly. This need combined with the requirement for effective online marketing operations will require a separate dedicated team.

I wish you good luck in your China online ventures. Remember that succeeding in the Chinese e-commerce market needs creativity, courage, and persistence. Whatever the product you want to sell, there are millions of Chinese consumers who would be willing to purchase it. Be decisive and make sure you do a thorough research before launching your product. Here is a short list of the main things any company needs to consider before entering the Chinese e-merging market:

- Take enough time to conduct a thorough market research.
- Consider hiring a quality service provider to set up and manage your online shop.
- Include Chinese in your website's language menu. This is crucial. Try to make it compatible with mobile platforms.
- Make sure you understand the whole process. A good logistics and distribution service is a determining success factor.
- Know your financial obligations.
- Carefully choose your brand name in Chinese. If you do not, your consumers will. Register your trademark with the local trademark bureau. The whole process will take one year to complete. You should normally obtain the certificate 12 months after the first approval.
- Be ready to have limited control over your IPR (intellectual property rights).
- Do not rely on a competitive price basis. Lower prices are important to Chinese consumers, but only unique and quality products will help you enter and stay in the Chinese e-commerce market.

- Make sure you provide the best customer service possible. Chinese e-shoppers are spoiled, in the sense that they expect immediate answers to their questions by means of an instant message.
- Be ready to deal with a lot of bureaucracy when it comes to obtaining licenses for certain product categories such as pharmaceuticals, medical devices, and food.
- Be aware that negative reviews will have a great impact on your overall merchant grade. Do everything you can to avoid them.
- Keep your existing customers engaged. Send out regular promotional information via SMS or e-mail.
- Do not forget how important it is to adapt your online and offline marketing strategy to match local practices and expectations.

List of things to consider:

Step 1 Research:

Market risks and opportunities
Product registration
Labeling requirements
Pricing
Warehousing
Supply chain

Step 2 Selling Online:

Choose an online platform
Choose and train the service provider
Create a flagship store
Align with local language website
Keep track of the competition
Monitor sales
Modify product or service offering and price if needed

Step 3 Getting your product into China:

Understand well regulations and product registration requirements
Hire an import agent
Monitor regulatory environment
Calculate customs fees and logistics costs

And, a few last tips:

Bargain!

Bargaining is an essential part of doing any form of business in China. It is only in international stores and big malls where people do not bargain. In all other situations, from the fruit market to the local clothes store, people do bargain. When I first arrived in China, I found this practice strange and rather exhausting because you have to go through it on several occasions daily. However, after some time, I got used to it, and I can hardly imagine living without it now! Bargaining is a daily ritual in China, and sellers do expect customers to bargain prices down. They will start with a somewhat high price, and as a customer, you are supposed to show discontent and complain about how expensive their product is. Then, you should offer a much lower price—unreasonably low sometimes—to finally set the price somewhere in the middle.

It is a funny ritual, and it allows you to buy things at a much lower price than you would pay in a mall store. The point is that both parties should have the feeling that it is a win–win deal. This is very important; otherwise, your Chinese customers will have the feeling of losing face, and this is something you should avoid by all means. In an e-commerce setting, Chinese customers usually bargain by complaining about a very high price, by trying to get the delivery of their purchase for free or by requesting some extra gift with the purchase. This leaves consumers with the feeling that they have a say in the whole buying process and the satisfaction that they have made a bargain.

Chinese consumers' fondness for bargaining explains why the C2C market share is bigger than the B2C market share in China. Because e-commerce bargaining takes place through instant messaging or text, a lack of direct communication would take away the possibility for your Chinese customers to try to bargain. For that reason, it is important to make sure that communication between you and your customers is interactive, and that they are given all the necessary tools to communicate with you about price matters in a fast and effective way.

Building a Unique Value Proposition

So far, few foreign companies have managed to successfully enter the Chinese e-merging market. Among the top 10 independent B2C e-merchants in 2012, there were only three foreign players: Amazon, Yihaodian (Walmart), and Newegg, with an online market share of 0.8, 0.4, and 0.2, respectively. Many foreign companies have failed in the past because they neglected to customize their offerings to local tastes and to offer something that is of real value to Chinese consumers. As China's e-commerce landscape is gaining in dynamics and complexity, foreign companies will need to create effective strategies in order to ensure a successful entry. Foreign e-tailers attempting their first entry in the Chinese e-merging market should be ready to suffer some initial losses. Many local companies have no unique value propositions to offer, but instead rely heavily on fierce price competition and sell the products at ridiculously low prices. This is not a viable option for foreign companies, and a unique selling point is necessary to differentiate your offering and stand out from the huge crowd of Chinese merchants.

Winning Customers Through Quality and Service

As consumers continually grow in number, they become increasingly demanding in terms of service and quality when shopping online. The near future will see a shift in demand from low- or average-quality products sold by dubious sources to higher-quality products sold by trustworthy merchants.

Market dynamics will remain challenging on the low-price front until local companies learn to compete on other levels than just price. You will need to define your online channel clearly, right from the start. Will your website be mainly a brand-building device? What will your distinctive value proposition be? Depending on the type of product or service you want to sell, there are different ways you can differentiate it from local competition. Product quality, product mix, brand reputation, and place of origin are the main areas foreign companies usually focus on to differentiate themselves. To state your company's unique selling point and ensure that the message gets clearly across to your customers, you will need to develop a new range of skills and assets on different fronts:

- Webstore design and usability: A user-friendly website with an appealing *look, touch, and feel* that is in harmony with the company's brand identity.
- Assortment strategy: A focused online product and assortment presentation based on an online fit assessment.
- Pricing strategy: Align across various channels and be inventive in order to reduce the chances or avoid online price battles.
- Service: Development of key service dimensions (such as payment options, delivery, after-service, or return terms) and level of service, which will have a tremendous impact on profitability.
- Traffic generation: Search engine marketing will be your key traffic driver. It will allow customers to easily reach you, and it will also allow your company to effectively reach out to attract new customers.
- Fulfillment and supply chain: Provide your customers with fast and efficient order processing, handling, and home delivery of goods.

I strongly encourage all of you to stay in the loop. Be open-minded and curious when working in China. Adapt to the latest technology and local social media trends. These changes, challenges, transitions, and catalysts are affecting China and the whole world. These are the skills the world will need for the coming decades to stay relevant and competitive in any field, especially when working in or with China.

Good luck with your China (ad)ventures!

2018 Digital China in Numbers

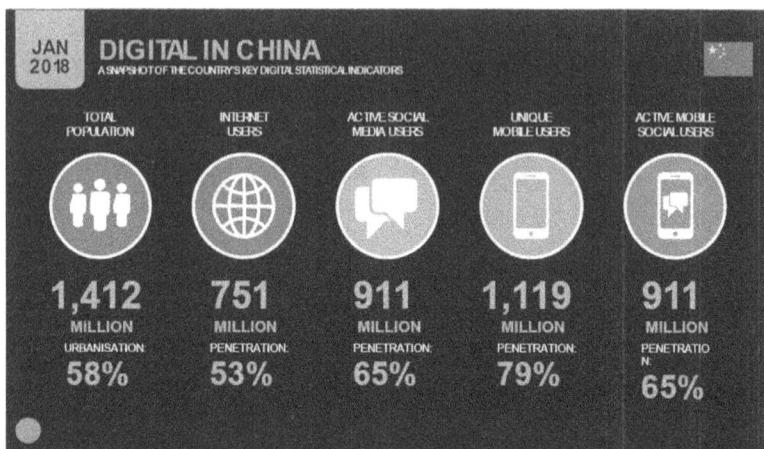

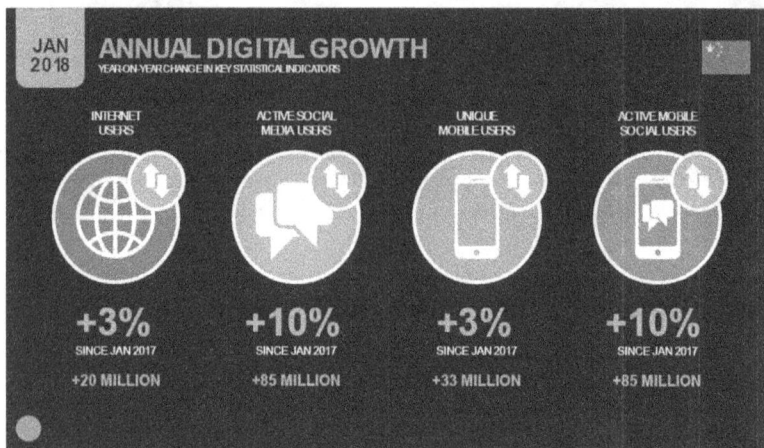

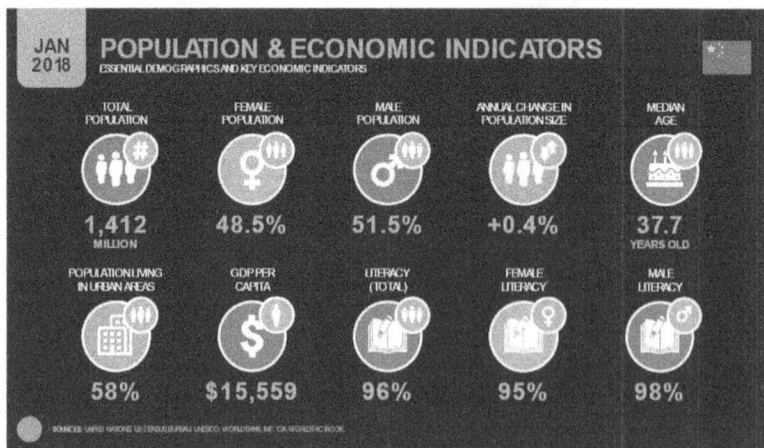

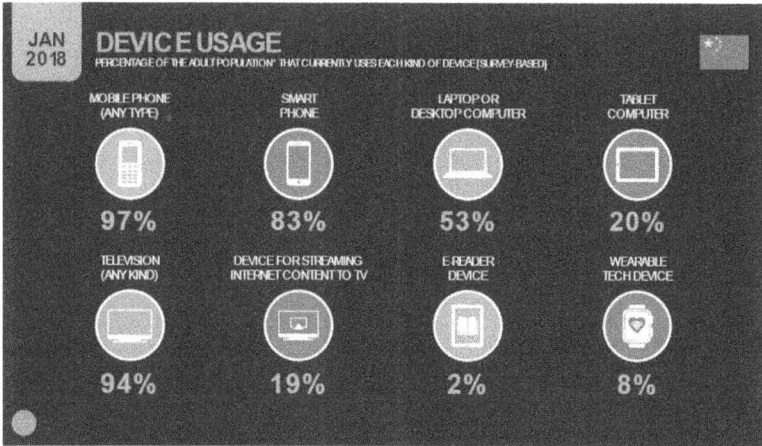

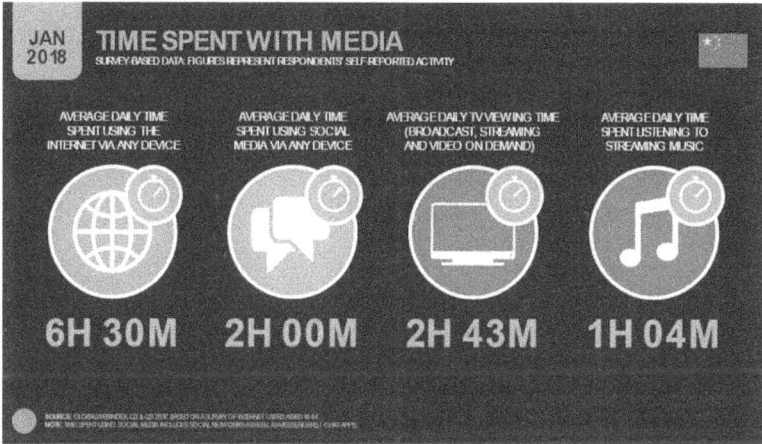

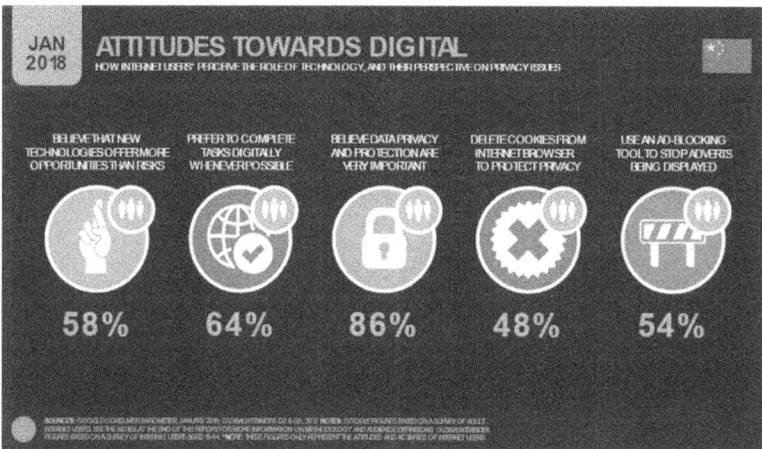

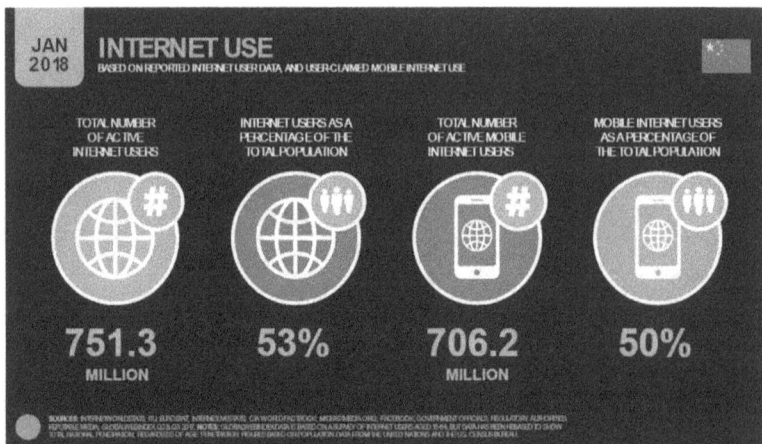

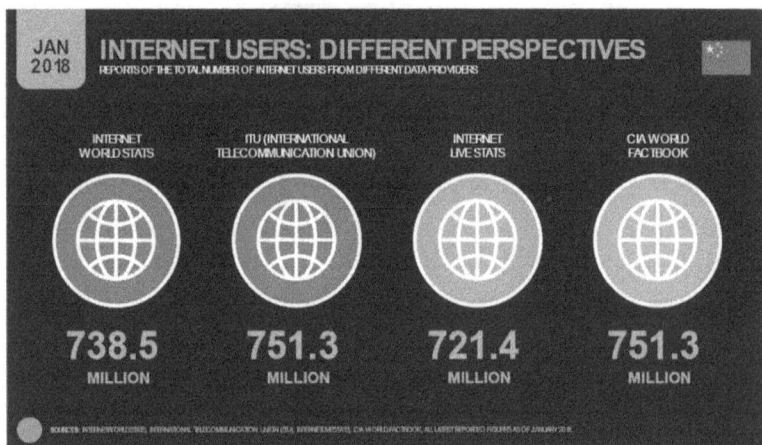

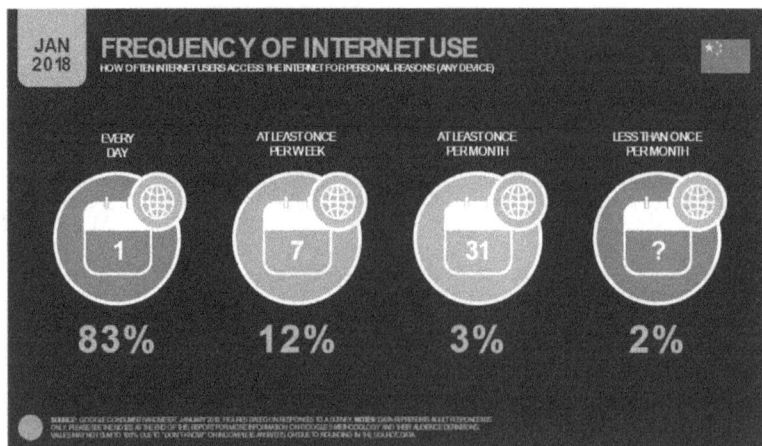

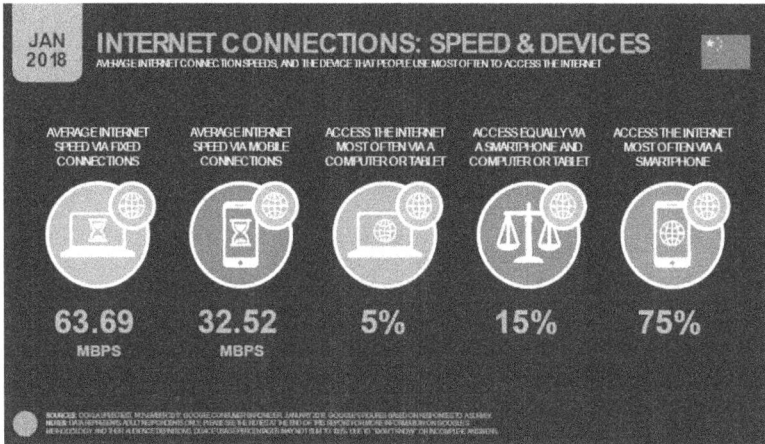

JAN 2018 — INTERNET CONNECTIONS: SPEED & DEVICES
AVERAGE INTERNET CONNECTION SPEEDS, AND THE DEVICE THAT PEOPLE USE MOST OFTEN TO ACCESS THE INTERNET

AVERAGE INTERNET SPEED VIA FIXED CONNECTIONS	AVERAGE INTERNET SPEED VIA MOBILE CONNECTIONS	ACCESS THE INTERNET MOST OFTEN VIA A COMPUTER OR TABLET	ACCESS EQUALLY VIA A SMARTPHONE AND COMPUTER OR TABLET	ACCESS THE INTERNET MOST OFTEN VIA A SMARTPHONE
63.69 MBPS	32.52 MBPS	5%	15%	75%

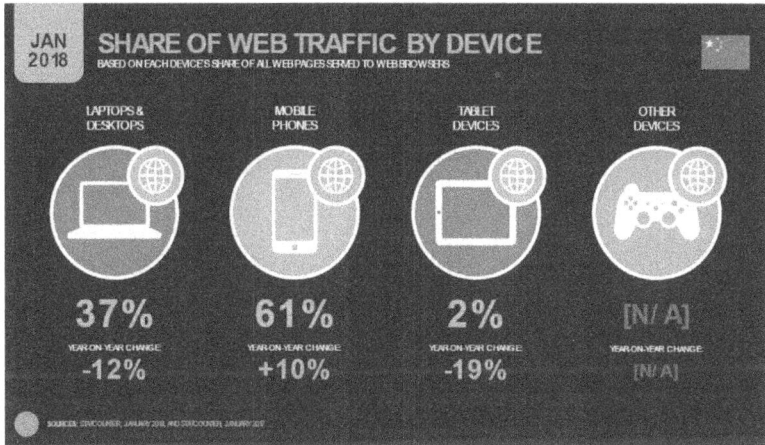

JAN 2018 — SHARE OF WEB TRAFFIC BY DEVICE
BASED ON EACH DEVICE'S SHARE OF ALL WEB PAGES SERVED TO WEB BROWSERS

LAPTOPS & DESKTOPS	MOBILE PHONES	TABLET DEVICES	OTHER DEVICES
37%	61%	2%	[N/A]
YEAR-ON-YEAR CHANGE -12%	YEAR-ON-YEAR CHANGE +10%	YEAR-ON-YEAR CHANGE -19%	YEAR-ON-YEAR CHANGE [N/A]

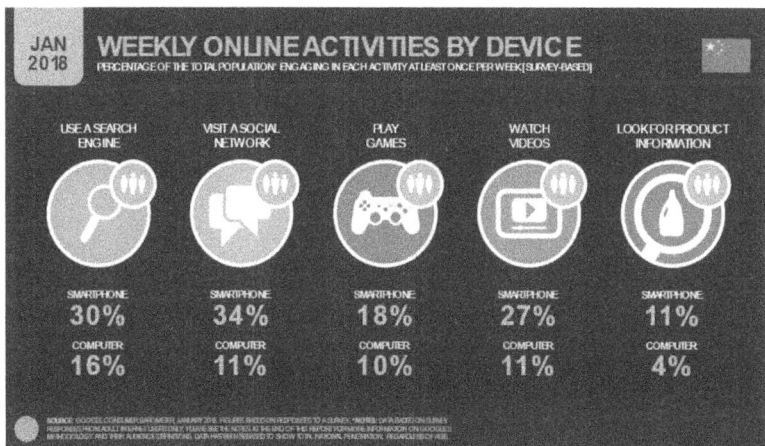

JAN 2018 — WEEKLY ONLINE ACTIVITIES BY DEVICE
PERCENTAGE OF THE TOTAL POPULATION ENGAGING IN EACH ACTIVITY AT LEAST ONCE PER WEEK (SURVEY-BASED)

USE A SEARCH ENGINE	VISIT A SOCIAL NETWORK	PLAY GAMES	WATCH VIDEOS	LOOK FOR PRODUCT INFORMATION
SMARTPHONE 30%	SMARTPHONE 34%	SMARTPHONE 18%	SMARTPHONE 27%	SMARTPHONE 11%
COMPUTER 16%	COMPUTER 11%	COMPUTER 10%	COMPUTER 11%	COMPUTER 4%

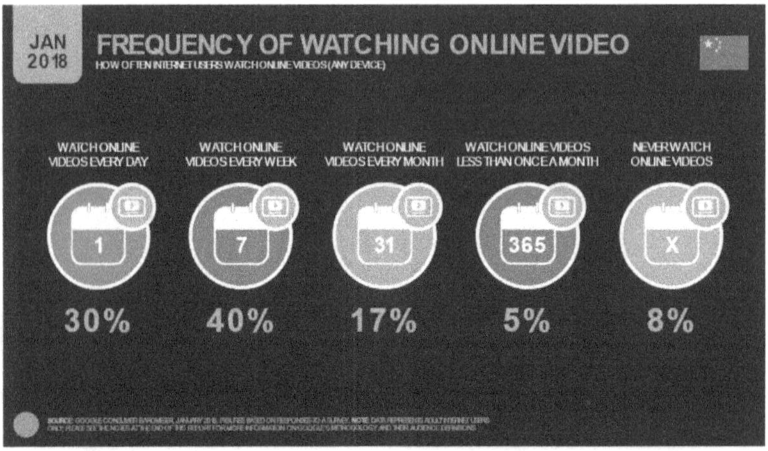
JAN 2018
FREQUENCY OF WATCHING ONLINE VIDEO
HOW OFTEN INTERNET USERS WATCH ONLINE VIDEOS (ANY DEVICE)
WATCH ONLINE VIDEOS EVERY DAY
WATCH ONLINE VIDEOS EVERY WEEK
WATCH ONLINE VIDEOS EVERY MONTH
WATCH ONLINE VIDEOS LESS THAN ONCE A MONTH
NEVER WATCH ONLINE VIDEOS
1
7
31
365
X
30%
40%
17%
5%
8%

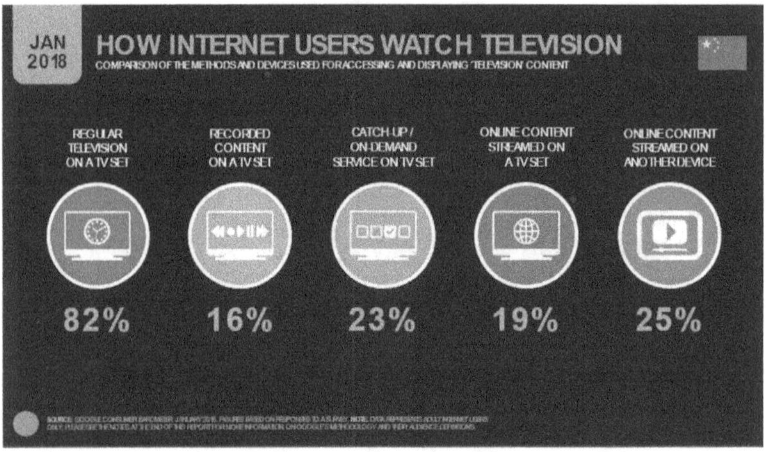
JAN 2018
HOW INTERNET USERS WATCH TELEVISION
COMPARISON OF THE METHODS AND DEVICES USED FOR ACCESSING AND DISPLAYING 'TELEVISION' CONTENT
REGULAR TELEVISION ON A TV SET
RECORDED CONTENT ON A TV SET
CATCH-UP / ON-DEMAND SERVICE ON TV SET
ONLINE CONTENT STREAMED ON A TV SET
ONLINE CONTENT STREAMED ON ANOTHER DEVICE
82%
16%
23%
19%
25%

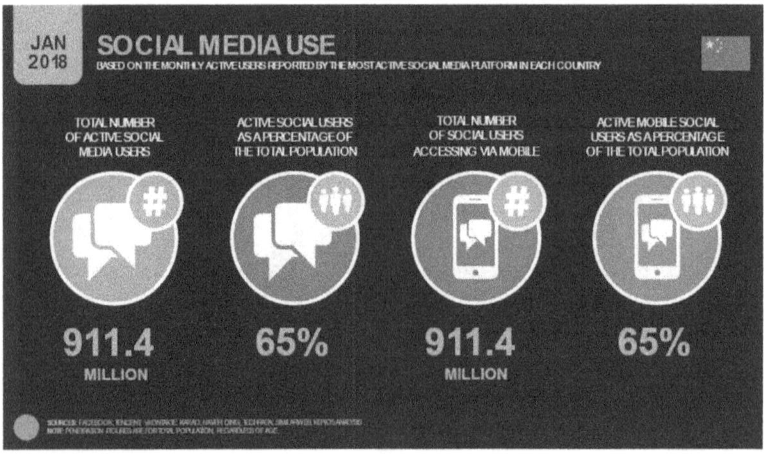
JAN 2018
SOCIAL MEDIA USE
BASED ON THE MONTHLY ACTIVE USERS REPORTED BY THE MOST ACTIVE SOCIAL MEDIA PLATFORM IN EACH COUNTRY
TOTAL NUMBER OF ACTIVE SOCIAL MEDIA USERS
ACTIVE SOCIAL USERS AS A PERCENTAGE OF THE TOTAL POPULATION
TOTAL NUMBER OF SOCIAL USERS ACCESSING VIA MOBILE
ACTIVE MOBILE SOCIAL USERS AS A PERCENTAGE OF THE TOTAL POPULATION
911.4
MILLION
65%
911.4
MILLION
65%

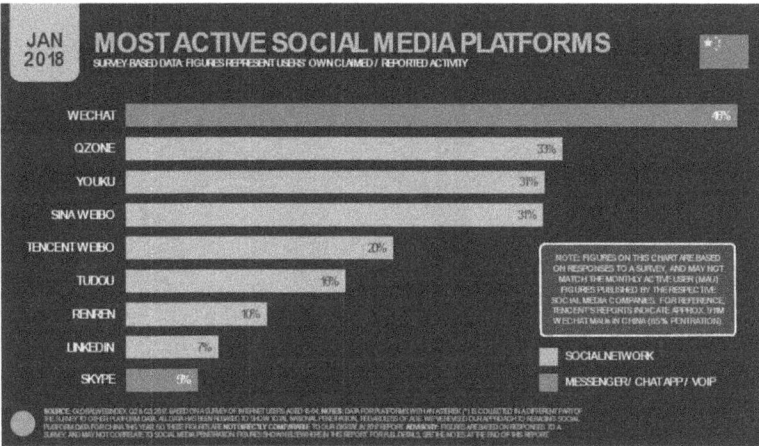

JAN 2018 — MOST ACTIVE SOCIAL MEDIA PLATFORMS

SURVEY-BASED DATA: FIGURES REPRESENT USERS' OWN CLAIMED / REPORTED ACTIVITY

- WECHAT — 47%
- QZONE — 33%
- YOUKU — 31%
- SINA WEIBO — 31%
- TENCENT WEIBO — 20%
- TUDOU — 18%
- RENREN — 10%
- LINKEDIN — 7%
- SKYPE — 7%

SOCIAL NETWORK
MESSENGER / CHAT APP / VOIP

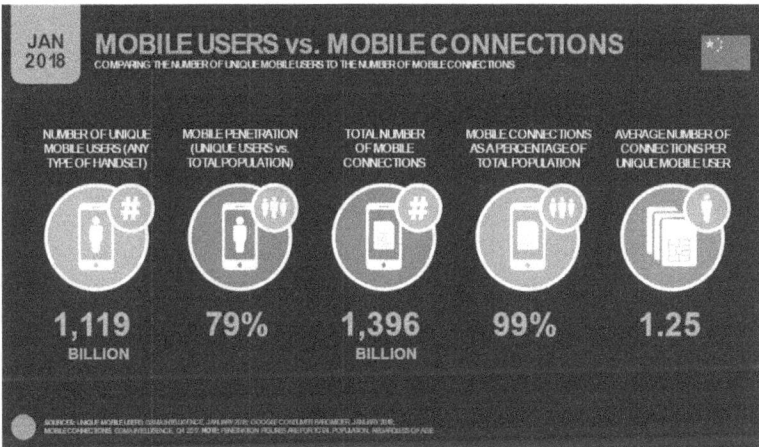

JAN 2018 — MOBILE USERS vs. MOBILE CONNECTIONS

COMPARING THE NUMBER OF UNIQUE MOBILE USERS TO THE NUMBER OF MOBILE CONNECTIONS

NUMBER OF UNIQUE MOBILE USERS (ANY TYPE OF HANDSET)	MOBILE PENETRATION (UNIQUE USERS vs. TOTAL POPULATION)	TOTAL NUMBER OF MOBILE CONNECTIONS	MOBILE CONNECTIONS AS A PERCENTAGE OF TOTAL POPULATION	AVERAGE NUMBER OF CONNECTIONS PER UNIQUE MOBILE USER
1,119 BILLION	79%	1,396 BILLION	99%	1.25

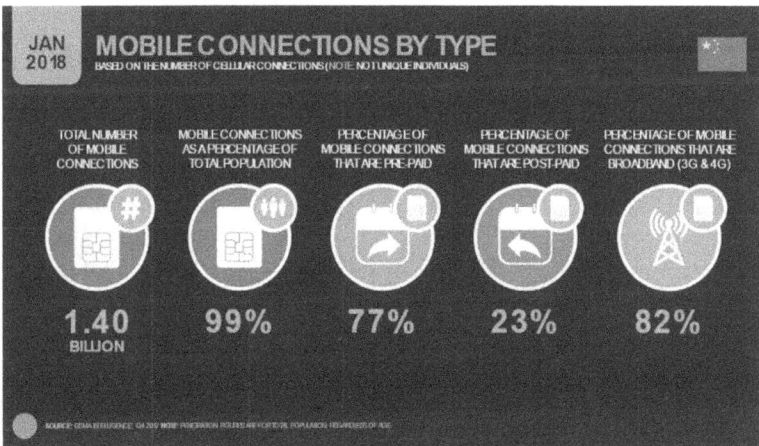

JAN 2018 — MOBILE CONNECTIONS BY TYPE

BASED ON THE NUMBER OF CELLULAR CONNECTIONS (NOTE: NOT UNIQUE INDIVIDUALS)

TOTAL NUMBER OF MOBILE CONNECTIONS	MOBILE CONNECTIONS AS A PERCENTAGE OF TOTAL POPULATION	PERCENTAGE OF MOBILE CONNECTIONS THAT ARE PRE-PAID	PERCENTAGE OF MOBILE CONNECTIONS THAT ARE POST-PAID	PERCENTAGE OF MOBILE CONNECTIONS THAT ARE BROADBAND (3G & 4G)
1.40 BILLION	99%	77%	23%	82%

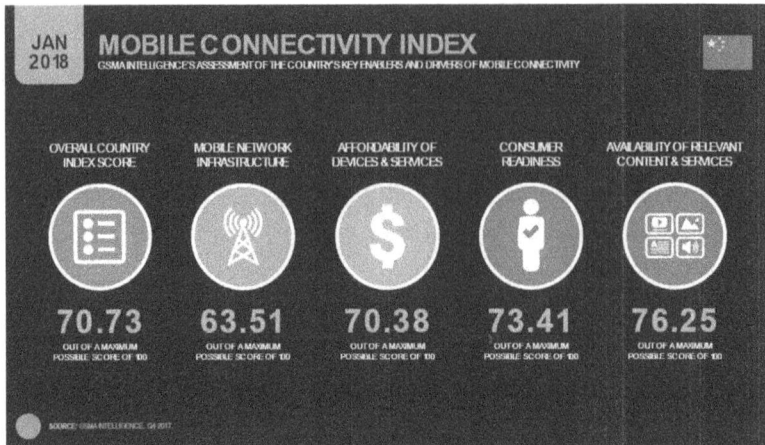

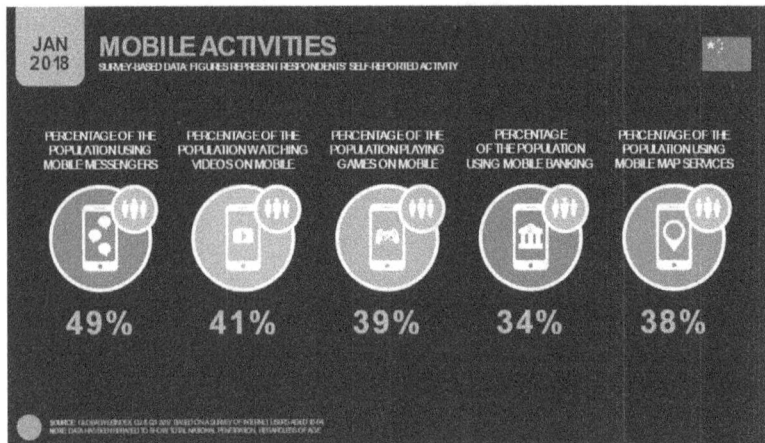

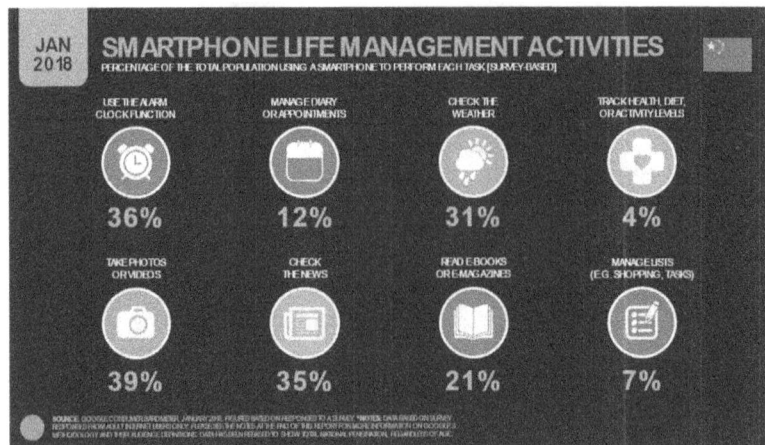

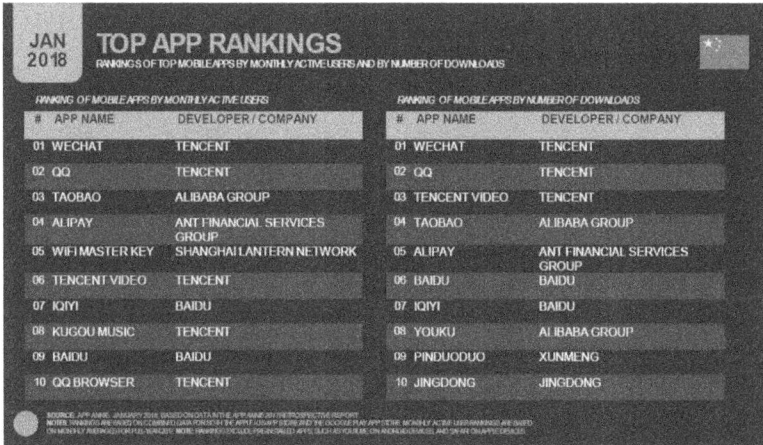

TOP APP RANKINGS
JAN 2018
RANKINGS OF TOP MOBILE APPS BY MONTHLY ACTIVE USERS AND BY NUMBER OF DOWNLOADS

RANKING OF MOBILE APPS BY MONTHLY ACTIVE USERS

#	APP NAME	DEVELOPER / COMPANY
01	WECHAT	TENCENT
02	QQ	TENCENT
03	TAOBAO	ALIBABA GROUP
04	ALIPAY	ANT FINANCIAL SERVICES GROUP
05	WIFI MASTER KEY	SHANGHAI LANTERN NETWORK
06	TENCENT VIDEO	TENCENT
07	IQIYI	BAIDU
08	KUGOU MUSIC	TENCENT
09	BAIDU	BAIDU
10	QQ BROWSER	TENCENT

RANKING OF MOBILE APPS BY NUMBER OF DOWNLOADS

#	APP NAME	DEVELOPER / COMPANY
01	WECHAT	TENCENT
02	QQ	TENCENT
03	TENCENT VIDEO	TENCENT
04	TAOBAO	ALIBABA GROUP
05	ALIPAY	ANT FINANCIAL SERVICES GROUP
06	BAIDU	BAIDU
07	IQIYI	BAIDU
08	YOUKU	ALIBABA GROUP
09	PINDUODUO	XUNMENG
10	JINGDONG	JINGDONG

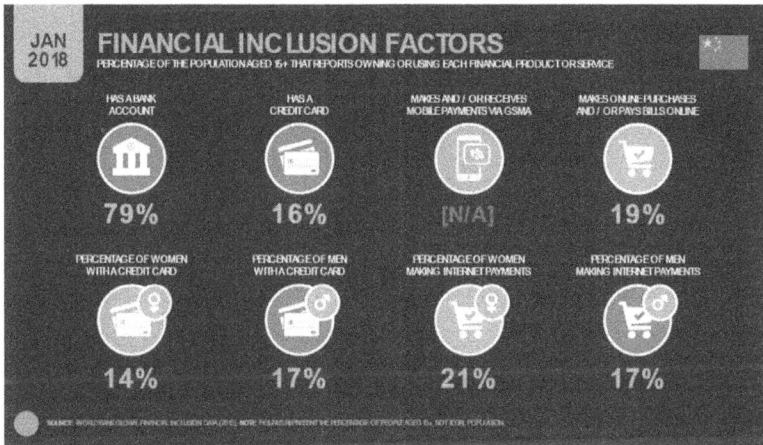

FINANCIAL INCLUSION FACTORS
JAN 2018
PERCENTAGE OF THE POPULATION AGED 15+ THAT REPORTS OWNING OR USING EACH FINANCIAL PRODUCT OR SERVICE

HAS A BANK ACCOUNT	HAS A CREDIT CARD	MAKES AND / OR RECEIVES MOBILE PAYMENTS VIA GSMA	MAKES ONLINE PURCHASES AND / OR PAYS BILLS ONLINE
79%	16%	[N/A]	19%

PERCENTAGE OF WOMEN WITH A CREDIT CARD	PERCENTAGE OF MEN WITH A CREDIT CARD	PERCENTAGE OF WOMEN MAKING INTERNET PAYMENTS	PERCENTAGE OF MEN MAKING INTERNET PAYMENTS
14%	17%	21%	17%

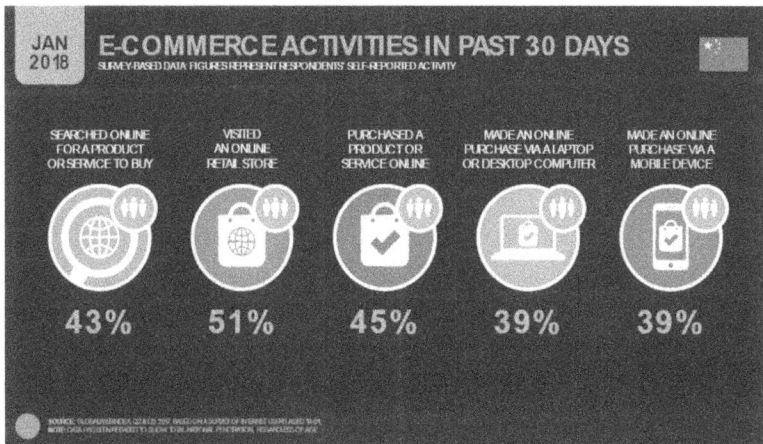

E-COMMERCE ACTIVITIES IN PAST 30 DAYS
JAN 2018
SURVEY-BASED DATA. FIGURES REPRESENT RESPONDENTS' SELF-REPORTED ACTIVITY

SEARCHED ONLINE FOR A PRODUCT OR SERVICE TO BUY	VISITED AN ONLINE RETAIL STORE	PURCHASED A PRODUCT OR SERVICE ONLINE	MADE AN ONLINE PURCHASE VIA A LAPTOP OR DESKTOP COMPUTER	MADE AN ONLINE PURCHASE VIA A MOBILE DEVICE
43%	51%	45%	39%	39%

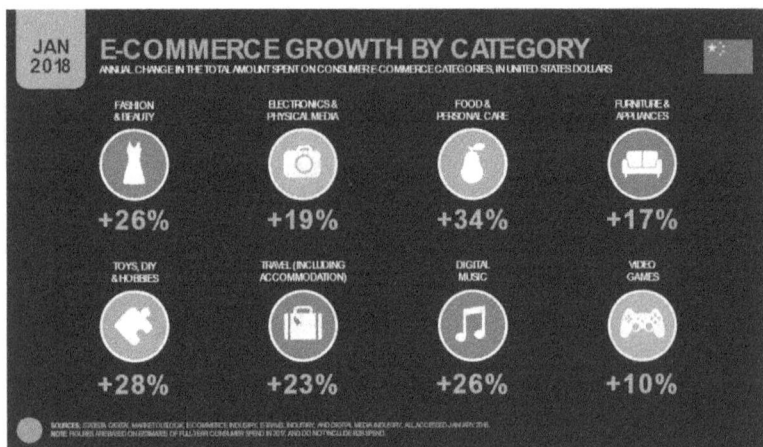

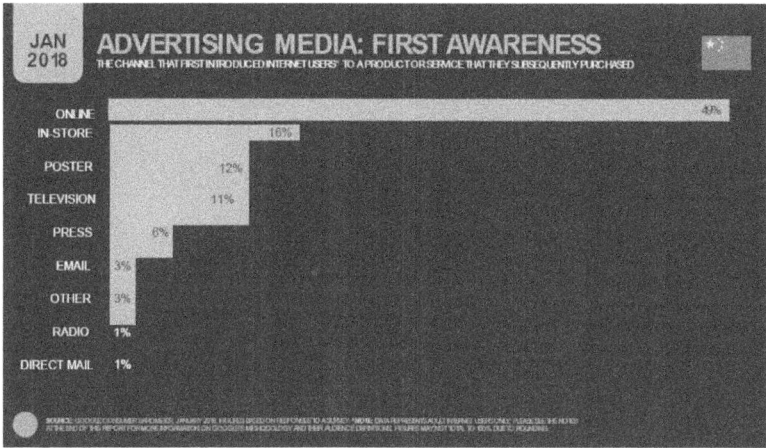

ADVERTISING MEDIA: FIRST AWARENESS

JAN 2018

THE CHANNEL THAT FIRST INTRODUCED INTERNET USERS' TO A PRODUCT OR SERVICE THAT THEY SUBSEQUENTLY PURCHASED

ONLINE	43%
IN-STORE	16%
POSTER	12%
TELEVISION	11%
PRESS	6%
EMAIL	3%
OTHER	3%
RADIO	1%
DIRECT MAIL	1%

Useful Links & References

- **Ministry of Information and Industry (MIIT)**
  The latest statistics on China's ICT and telecommunications industries from the Chinese government.
  www.miit.gov.cn
- **China Internet Network Information Centre**
  The latest statistics on internet usage in China.
  http://cnnic.net.cn/en/index/
- **European Union Chamber Of Commerce In China**
  www.eusmecenter.org
- **Amcham/American Chamber Of Commerce In China**
  www.amchamchina.org
- **China-Britain Business Council**
  http://cbbc.org/
- **Mc Kinsey Global Institute Analysis**
  www.mckinsey.com
- **Iresearch China**
  www.iresearchchina.com
- **China Internet Watch**
  www.chinainternetwatch.com
- **Fung Business Intelligence Center**
  www.fungfroup.com
- **At Kearney Consulting**
  www.atkearney.com
- **China Briefing**
  www.china-briefing.com

Bibliography

Alibaba Group. 2017. *Company Overview*. Alibaba Group.

Engel, J.F., P.W. Miniard, and R.D. Blackwell. 2006. *Consumer Behavior*, 10th ed. USA: Thomson South-Western, Mason.

Chen, A., and V. Vishwanath. 2005. "Expanding in China." *Harvard Business Review* 83, no. 3, pp. 19–21.

China Union Pay. 2018. *Overview Union Pay*. China Union Pay.

CIA – The World Factbook. 2017. China, Central Intelligence Agency.

CNNIC. 2018. *Internet Statistics*. China Internet Network Information Center.

Corbitt, B.J., T. Thanasankit, and H. Yi. 2003. "Trust and E-commerce: A Study of Consumer Perceptions." *Electronic Commerce Research and Applications* 2, no. 3, pp. 203–15.

Creswell, J.W. 1994. *Research Design: Qualitative, Quantitative, and Mixed Methods Approaches*. California: Sage Publications.

Custodio, E.T. 2004. "E-commerce: The Work Program of the World Trade Organization." In *The New Economy in East Asia and the Pacific*, ed. P. Drysdale, 1st ed. Oxon: Routledge Curzon.

Demil, B., and X. Lecocq. 2010. "Business Model Evolution: In Search of Consistency." *Long Range Planning* 43, nos. 2–3, pp. 227–46.

Determann, L., and A. Marson. 2009. "Internet Business Law in China for US Companies." *The Computer and Internet Lawyer* 26, no. 4, pp. 13–18.

Douglas, D. 2003. "Inductive Theory Generation: A Grounded Approach to Business Inquiry." *Electronic Journal of Business Research Methods* 2, no. 1, pp. 47–54.

Dubosson-Torbay, M., A. Osterwalder, and Y. Pigneur. 2002. "E-business Model Design, Classification, and Measurements." *Thunderbird International Business Review* 44, no. 1, pp. 5–23.

Dunford, R., I. Palmer, and J. Benveniste. 2010. "Business Model Replication for Early and Rapid Internationalisation." *Long Range Planning* 43, nos. 2–3, pp. 655–74.

Dyer, G.W., and A.L. Wilkins. 1991. "Better Stories, Not Better Constructs, to Generate Better Theory: A Rejoinder to Eisenhardt." *Academy of Management Review* 16, no. 3, pp. 613–19.

Eisenhardt, K.M. 1989. "Building Theories from Case Study Research." *Academy of Management Review* 14, no. 4, pp. 532–50.

Eko, L., A. Kumar, and Y. Qingjiang. 2011. "Google This: The Great Firewall of China, The IT wheel of India, Google Inc., and Internet Regulation." *Journal of Internet Law* 15, no. 3, pp. 3–14.

Eriksson, P., and A. Kovalainen. 2008. *Qualitative Methods in Business Research*, 1st ed. Los Angeles, USA: Sage Publication Ltd.

Farrell, D., U. Gersch, and E. Stephenson. 2006. "The McKinsey Quarterly: The value of China's Emerging Middle Class. [brochure]." *McKinsey Quarterly 2*, no. 1, p. 60.

Hair, J.F. Jr., A.H. Money, P. Samouel, and M. Page. 2007. *Research Methods For Business*, 1st ed. Hoboken: John Wiley & Sons Ltd.

Hall, E.T. 1959. *The Silent Language*, 1st ed. New York: NY: Doubleday.

Hanover Research. 2013. "Social and Web Marketing in China Report."

Hedman, J., and T. Kalling. 2001. "The Business Model: A Means to Understand the Business Context of Information and Communication Technology." Working paper. Lund, Sweden: School of Economics and Management Lund University.

Hille, K. 2011. "Taobao Mall in Ecommerce Alliance." *The Financial Times*. http://ft.com/intl/cms/s/0/1f1efc3e-e2b3-11e0-897a-00144feabdc0.html#axzz1ohwps6OI [retrieved: 2012-03-10]

Hofstede, G., G.J. Hofstede, and M. Minkov. 2010. *Cultures and Organizations–Software of the Mind*, 3rd ed. United States: McGraw-Hill.

Hultén, P., J. Hultman, and L.T. Eriksson. 2007. *Kritiskt Tänkande*, 1st ed. Malmö, Sweden: Liber.

Ilayperuma, T. 2010, *Improving E-business Design Through Business Model Analysis* (Doctoral Thesis). Stockholm, Sweden: Department of Computer and Systems Science Stockholm University.

Johnson, M.W., C.M. Christensen, and H. Kagermann. 2008. "Reinventing Your Business Model." *Harvard Business Review* 86, no. 12, pp. 50–59.

Laudon, K.C., and C.G. Traver. 2011. *E-commerce: Business Technology Society*, 7th ed. New Jersey: Prentice Hall.

Lewis, R.D. 2000a. *When Cultures Collide: Managing Successfully Across Cultures*, 2nd ed. London, UK: Nicholas Brealey.

Linder, J., and S. Cantrell. 2000. "Changing Business Models: Surveying the Landscape." *Accenture Institute for Strategic Change*. Working Paper.

Liao, H., R.W. Proctor, and G. Salvendy. 2009. "Chinese and US Online Consumers' Preference for Content of E-commerce Websites: A Survey." *Theoretical Issues in Ergonomics Science* 10, no. 1, pp. 19–42.

Liu, X., M. He, F. Gao, and P. Xie. 2008. "An Empirical Study of Online Shopping Customer Satisfaction in China: A Holistic Perspective." *International Journal of Retail and Distribution Management* 36, no. 11, pp. 919–40.

Lu, P.X. 2008. *Elite China: Luxury Consumer Behavior in China*, 1st ed. Singapore: John Wiley & Sons (Asia) Pte. Ltd.

Lu, P.X., and M. Chevalier. 2010. *Luxury China: Market Opportunities and Potentials*, 1st ed. Singapore: John Wiley & Sons Asia Pte. Ltd.

Maslow, A.H. 1943. "A Theory of Human Motivation." *Psychological Review* 50, no. 4, pp. 370–96.

Maverick China Research. 2012. "China 20/20: The Future of Mobile Payment in China."

McKinsey Global Institute. 2013. "China Online Retail Sector Report."

Selling Online in China. 2012. "EU SME Center Report."

About the Author

Danai Krokou was born in Corfu, a Greek island in the Ionian Sea. She left her hometown at age 17 to study and work in numerous countries around the world. She is an international business development consultant, Chinese market investment specialist, entrepreneur, and passionate polyglot. She studied in France, the United Kingdom, Spain, Denmark, and China. She majored in French Language and Literature, International Politics and Business. She is fluent in seven languages including Mandarin Chinese. She started her first business at age 25 in Shanghai, China and is one of the youngest female entrepreneurs in Asia. She is the author of *Power Quotes: For Life, Business, and Leadership* published by Business Expert Press. She has also authored a series of advisory books aimed at American and European SMEs and entrepreneurs who seek to understand and ideally enter the Chinese market.

For more information visit: www.danaikrokou.com

Index

OTHER TITLES IN THE INTERNATIONAL BUSINESS COLLECTION

Tamer Cavusgil, Georgia State; Michael Czinkota, Georgetown;
and Gary Knight, Willamette University, Editors

- *Creative Solutions to Global Business Negotiations, Second Edition* by Claude Cellich and Jain Subhash
- *Doing Business in Russia: A Concise Guide, Volume I* by Anatoly Zhuplev
- *Doing Business in Russia: A Concise Guide, Volume II* by Anatoly Zhuplev
- *Major Sociocultural Trends Shaping the Contemporary World* by K.H. Yeganeh
- *Globalization Alternatives: Strategies for the New International Economy* by Joseph Mark Munoz
- *Doing Business in the United States: A Guide for Small Business Entrepreneurs with a Global Mindset* by Anatoly Zhuplev, Matthew Stefl, and Andrew Rohm
- *In Search for the Soul of International Business* by Michael R. Czinkota

Announcing the Business Expert Press Digital Library

Concise e-books business students need for classroom and research

This book can also be purchased in an e-book collection by your library as

- a one-time purchase,
- that is owned forever,
- allows for simultaneous readers,
- has no restrictions on printing, and
- can be downloaded as PDFs from within the library community.

Our digital library collections are a great solution to beat the rising cost of textbooks. E-books can be loaded into their course management systems or onto student's e-book readers. The **Business Expert Press** digital libraries are very affordable, with no obligation to buy in future years. For more information, please visit **www.businessexpertpress.com/librarians**. To set up a trial in the United States, please email **sales@businessexpertpress.com**.

www.ingramcontent.com/pod-product-compliance
Lightning Source LLC
Chambersburg PA
CBHW070522200326
41519CB00013B/2896